THE
FAIRY
PARTY
BOOK

The Fairy Party Book

Bringing Magic into Every Celebration Throughout the Year

Marina T. Stern

Red Wheel
Boston, MA / York Beach, ME

First published in 2003 by
Red Wheel/Weiser, LLC
York Beach, ME

With offices at:
368 Congress Street
Boston, MA 02210
www.redwheelweiser.com

Library of Congress Cataloging-in-Publication Data
Stern, Marina T.
   The fairy party book : bringing magic into every celebration throughout the year /
Marina T. Stern.
         p. cm.
   ISBN 1-59003-054-0
   1. Holidays. 2. Holiday cookery. I. Title.
   GT3930S74 2003
   394.26--dc21

                                                                        2003010017

Typeset in Adobe Garamond by Kathleen Wilson Fivel

Printed in Canada
TCP

10 09 08 07 06 05 04 03
8 7 6 5 4 3 2 1

FOR SHARON JOHNSON,
WHO HAS PROVEN HER WORTH
AGAIN AND AGAIN.

CONTENTS

ACKNOWLEDGMENTS

The first person I must thank, for putting me on the path to making this book a reality, is Robyn Heisey, Associate Publisher at Red Wheel/Weiser. The book was her inspiration, plain and simple. She has been generous with her ideas and encouragement beyond all expectations. Who else could request a rewrite with such charm that I could hardly wait to get back to work? If this book has any value, it is a direct result of her suggestions. Bless you, Robyn.

My husband, Tom Stern, has supported me in every possible way. Beside providing room and board, hugs and kisses, screening my phone calls, and rearranging his schedule to accommodate my writing plans, he provides live-in technical support for my computer. As a long-time folklorist, ordained minister, and hospice nurse, I find matters of life and death much less mysterious than the plastic box on my desk. Bless you, Tom.

Sharon Johnson, with her kind heart and sly humor, has given of her friendship. She has also given me free access to her extensive collection of ethnic and historic cookbooks, which has greatly enriched the content of this book. Long life and happiness to you, my friend.

All the people who have entertained me in their homes have contributed to this work: Dan Brogan, Jeffrey Dangermond, Noel Wolfman, and others who have requested that I not use their names. In addition, I have to thank all the people who have been my guests. A host without a guest is just a lonely guy with too much food in the house.

INTRODUCTION

Everyone in the world likes to party. Everyone in the world *needs* to party. In my research, I have found some of the most riotous celebrations embedded in the most somber cultures. Perhaps stolid, hard-working folk especially need to go wild, in order to bring balance to their lives.

What we celebrate defines who we are. Whom we entertain defines whom we love, and where we belong. Whether you celebrate Chanukah, or Solstice, or Christmas tells volumes about you-and if you celebrate them all, that tells even more. With whom do you spend Thanksgiving? Love them or hate them, the people you see across the turkey on the fourth Thursday in November are your family. Whether the bonds are made by blood, marriage, or shared memories matters little. Where is your heart, when you are baking batch after batch of cookies, or sipping cocoa by the fire? This is your home.

The Gentle Folk share our homes, lurk in the corners and under the shrubs. Note that it is unlucky to call these Gentle People of Celtic lore "fairies," as they consider the term demeaning. I recognize no such taboo around the word "elf," and its derivatives to refer to the beings of lands farther north. Whatever its former connotations may have been, the popularity of the works of J. R. R. Tolkien over the last half century has made "elvish" the highest compliment the English language has to offer.

The Gentle Folk are present at our entertainments as well. They revel in our music, share in our feasts, giggle at our amours. In earlier days, we paid more attention to them, but lately we have neglected them. As our activities have changed from agriculture to manufacturing to the exchange of information, we have forgotten our ancient friends. Sadly, what we have lost in the depths of our roots, we have not made up in breadth of experience.

My intent in this volume is to reacquaint you with some of the old ways, of different ways around the world, and of the place the Fair Folk once had in our celebrations.

There are no guard stations at the borders of the realm of Faerie. The inhabitants come and go at will, appearing now in the guise of an insect or a bird, another time as a legendary hero. The Folk can appear as gods, demigods, or saints. For example, Bridget, also known as Brigid or Bride, started her career as a goddess associated with wells and springs. She was dubbed a saint at the time of the Christianization of Ireland. She was not entirely tamed at that time, however, as she took a third identity as a queen among the Good Folk.

The realm of Faerie encompasses oceans as well as lakes, streams, and wells. It comprises natural rockfalls as well as ancient and mysterious standing stones, abandoned buildings as well as inhabited ones, meadows and woodlands as well as modern cities. The denizens of Faerie include seals that can become human, water horses that eat human flesh, and women more beautiful than human women. If you have ever overheard laughter in a lonely place, but could not find its source, you have heard one of the Folk.

The "fairies" seen in children's book illustrations-presented as pretty girls no more than four inches tall, with the wings of a butterfly or dragonfly-represent only a small subset of the residents of Faerie. All things that stand on the cusp of belief and imagination are parts of Faerie. People talk of computer "bugs." There is a common belief that the term goes back to the days of punch cards. A small insect blocked the hole in a punch card, causing a malfunction. While that may be the reason this particular sprite is called a "bug," the idea, and the word, go back centuries. "Bug" is an old term referring to a mischievous spirit. It is related to "boggle," "bogie," and "bugbear." In addition, the demeanor of a person whose computer is acting up is not neutral, as might be expected if a hand tool had broken. People whose computers are "buggy" speak and act as if the source of the problem were a mischievous or even malevolent being, who must be banished or appeased.

What does any of this have to do with throwing parties? Only that the Folk are fascinated by us. If we pay attention to our computers, then so (unfortunately!) will they. Many of them love us; many others do not. It seems that most of them seek our company at one time or another, although those who approach us may not be a representative sample. After all, we will neither know nor suspect any beings that succeed in avoiding us utterly.

The purpose of celebrating milestones and holidays in traditional ways is manifold. It strengthens bonds within families, friendship groups, and communities. It draws benevolent entities into our circle of acquaintance, which in turn increases our chances for success and happiness. It repels malevolent spirits, providing some protection against unfavorable strokes of fortune. Finally, celebrating our occasions in traditional ways can influence ambivalent beings to favor us.

As one example, take the case of the brownies and the boggles. Brownies are friendly sprites who help with the housework, befriend the livestock, and generally bring good luck. Boggles can range from annoying to deadly. In minor cases, they spill the flour and break the plates. In serious cases, they cause disease, fire, and miscarriage. *Brownies and boggles are the same beings.* How they behave depends on how they have been treated by the human beings with whom they share their dwellings. If leaving a piece of cake and a glass of milk by the fire will encourage them to behave like brownies rather than boggles, then do it.

Some may ask why we should be concerned with such things. Is it not just a bunch of superstitions? Let me tell you a story.

Once upon a time, there was a people who had a complicated set of taboos related to using marmots (woodchucks) as a meat animal. It was forbidden to catch marmots in a trap. It was forbidden to shoot one, if it was sluggish or acting strangely. It was forbidden to come close to a marmot that had died of natural causes. These taboos had been in place for as long as anyone could remember, and no one knew why they had been instituted in the beginning.

Another people moved into the land, a people who prided themselves on their high civilization and their freedom from superstition. They treated marmots as they treated any other animal that could be hunted for meat. They trapped them. They shot them without regard to their behavior. Once in a while, they might even skin one they found dead, in order to use its fur. The people sickened and died, and their disease spread throughout the known world.

This really happened. The place was northern Asia; the disease was bubonic plague. You may have heard of the epidemic that was started by the flouting of old superstitions; history records it as the Black Death. Plague had been endemic in Asia since the time beyond memory. The native peoples of the area had developed a series of behaviors that prevented them from being exposed to the fleas of plague-infested rodents, millennia before anyone knew that rodents carried plague or that fleas spread it. Their superstitions saved their lives.

I do not suspect that any of the traditions I recount here has any similar life-preserving qualities. Most probably do little more than evoke long-buried memories. Still, what is consciousness, if not a continuous stream of memories? A deeper awareness of one's own traditions anchors one more strongly to the earth, and a wider understanding of other traditions helps strengthen one against the stress caused by too-rapid change. In this century, in this country and many others, we are not born in the home in which we will live out our lives. Our hometowns and our old friends can become a distant memory, as we follow our careers from boomtown to boomtown. Those who are deeply and broadly rooted in tradition are better equipped to maintain their selfhood in the face of the erosive dehumanization of modern life.

And yes, those who know how to throw a good party will have more friends than those who do not. These friends, whether in the waking world or the shadowy land of Faerie, will give them comfort in hard times, and delight in good ones.

I have drawn on the traditions of many lands, for interest as well diversity. I have never heard of an attack by the Yule Cat in North America. It probably poses no genuine threat outside Iceland, but the story is too good to leave out. Many peoples have settled here, bringing with them their customs, their beliefs, and their accompanying spirits. May they all be well entertained.

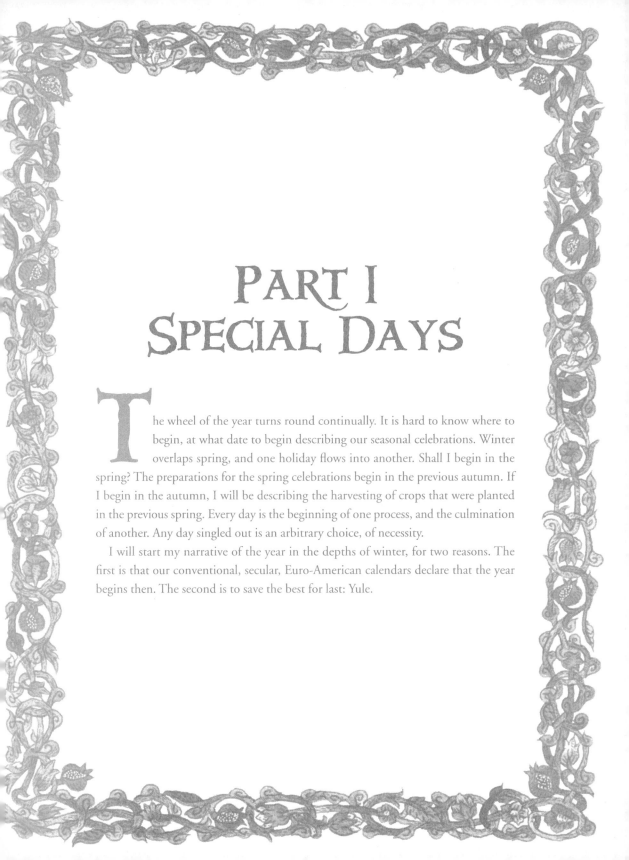

PART I
SPECIAL DAYS

The wheel of the year turns round continually. It is hard to know where to begin, at what date to begin describing our seasonal celebrations. Winter overlaps spring, and one holiday flows into another. Shall I begin in the spring? The preparations for the spring celebrations begin in the previous autumn. If I begin in the autumn, I will be describing the harvesting of crops that were planted in the previous spring. Every day is the beginning of one process, and the culmination of another. Any day singled out is an arbitrary choice, of necessity.

I will start my narrative of the year in the depths of winter, for two reasons. The first is that our conventional, secular, Euro-American calendars declare that the year begins then. The second is to save the best for last: Yule.

CHAPTER I
NEW YEAR'S EVE
NEW YEAR'S DAY
December 31, January 1

In the tradition of many cultures worldwide, let us begin the day at sunset, rather than at midnight. Many holidays are primarily celebrated on the night before. New Year is among these. If we start New Year at midnight, we miss the party.

Here in the United States, the chief traditions are to dress up in formal wear, attend elegant parties, drink too much champagne, and kiss various members of the opposite sex at midnight. These indiscriminate kisses are remnants of the sexual license of Saturnalia, the favorite holiday of demigods and other supernatural beings for thousands of years. We will speak of Saturnalia later.

Americans attach great importance to having a date on New Year's Eve. Being alone is considered an omen of continued loneliness, and visible evidence of low status. Further, one's companion on New Year's Eve should be a serious prospect, not a casual date. The stress of finding just the right date on New Year's Eve is such that newly engaged couples are frequently told, "Now you will always have a date for New Year's Eve," no matter what time of year they make the announcement.

For those unwilling to participate in the circus of formal parties and obligatory romance, the tradition is to stay up until midnight in front of the TV, watching the public celebrations in New York. If you have someone special to kiss at midnight, this arrangement can be just as satisfactory as going out.

If the kissing leads to canoodling, you may hear the Folk, giggling from behind the headboard.

On New Year's Day, the tradition is to have a hangover from the excessive champagne consumed the night before. If one has been so imprudent as to give the first kiss at midnight to someone other than one's own spouse, a chilly greeting is also traditional. Once these have been gotten out of the way, the tradition is to watch parades, either in person or on television. We also resolve to improve ourselves, by breaking all of our bad habits.

Human nature being what it is, all of these resolutions are to be abandoned by Twelfth Night, which is January 6. If we were to succeed in banishing our foibles, we would bore the Folk right out of our lives.

Some regions have celebratory foods associated with New Year's Day. In the southern states, people eat black-eyed peas for luck, either plain or combined with rice to make Hoppin' John. Doing so brings luck and prosperity for the coming year. Luck is in the domain of the Folk. Anything that we do "for luck" we are actually doing to gain the favor of the Folk.

Farther afield, traditions vary.

In Germany, as in the U.S., the tradition is to throw parties and stay up past midnight. They have the added incentive of fireworks at midnight to give them a reason to stay awake. Fireworks were invented in China, and first used there to frighten away evil spirits. The wonder and joy with which human crowds watch fireworks are just as effective in attracting benevolent beings.

For luck, Germans throw an egg over the house, and bury it where it falls. This is most effective for people with small houses and strong throwing arms. For others, the effects are indistinguishable from the Halloween custom of egging houses. Germans also believe that those who eat smoked pork chops and sauerkraut on New Year's Day will have plenty of money all year.

New Year is the most important holiday in Japan, and is celebrated for three days. As with many traditional holiday celebrations, the women take this opportunity to clean their houses from top to bottom. Japanese people decorate their front doorsteps. In their entryways, they place giant rice cakes and tangerines, which they will eat with their families when the holiday ends. They display other symbols of prosperity as well, such as ferns, oranges, and lobsters. The host of Folk take notice, and provide the householders with the real prosperity that the decorations symbolize.

New Year's Eve / New Year's Day

The Japanese send cards to everyone they know, much as we do at our most important holidays. Children visit all their relatives, who give them money. As we do, the Japanese resolve to break all their bad habits. They fly kites, spin tops, and play cards and board games. They ring the temple bells 108 times, to drive off evil influences for the coming year.

Indonesians consider it important to make a lot of noise on New Year's Eve, with paper trumpets and other devices. As Indonesia is predominantly Moslem, they change the date for the New Year's festivities if December 31 falls during a Moslem fast. The Folk are flexible, and will as soon attend a party on one day as on another.

In Finland, people tell fortunes on New Year's Eve by dropping small amounts of molten tin into a bucket of cold water. With skill, they read the future in the shadows cast by the irregular pieces of tin. All fortune-telling activities involve the Folk, as foretelling the future involves pulling aside the curtain that separates our realm from the timeless land of Faerie.

In Puerto Rico, people consider it vital to clean not only their houses but their cars, and even the streets in front of their homes. They believe that, in whatever condition the stroke of midnight finds their property, that's the way it will remain for the next year.

For luck, Puerto Ricans eat one grape at each stroke of the clock at midnight. This tradition comes from Spain, and is common to many Spanish-speaking countries. It is more difficult than it sounds. When the clock has finished striking, people run outside and honk their car horns. In other parts of Latin America, people welcome the New Year by firing pistols into the air. This leads to the complementary custom of huddling indoors for safety. As a confirmed huddler, I prefer the honking of horns. The noise is not used to drive off evil spirits, but is considered festive in its own right. No one may avoid the celebration by sleeping.

After midnight, there is a celebratory feast. This is not unusually late, as the custom in most cultures that derive from Spain is to eat dinner after 10:00 P.M., even on school nights. The Folk in Spain behave much like the Folk in France and Germany, with whom we have been familiar since childhood, when we heard European "fairy" tales. Remember the stories of Cinderella, of Beauty and the Beast. These Folk enjoy late nights, fine food, and dancing.

In Cuba, in addition to the customs cited for Puerto Rico, children build scarecrows, which they keep on their front porches during the day. At midnight, they take the scarecrows outside and burn them. Wildness, anarchy, and danger are also attributes of the Folk worldwide. This is something we have in common with them, in the secret cores of our hearts.

In Mallorca, an island off the coast of Spain, families have a festive dinner together before midnight. They watch the festivities in Madrid on the TV, toasting the stroke of midnight with Spanish bubbly. Then the old folks and the children turn in, while those of a dancing disposition go out to party until dawn. In many circumstances, the Folk seek out the company of old people, who are full of stories and wisdom, or of children, who are innocent and open to new experiences. On New Year's Eve, the Folk would rather go *dancing*.

In Orkney, between Scotland and Greenland, young men in masks go from house to house, singing. Householders reward them for their efforts with food and beer. Because of the masks, the householders do not know whether the singers are their own neighbors or magical beings, with the power to bless or blast. The Folk are numerous in Orkney, and powerful.

There are many fairy traditions related to New Year's Eve in Iceland. The people believe that on New Year's Eve cows can talk, seals take human form, and the dead rise from their graves. If they have never witnessed these events, it is because of a taboo regarding nosiness. It is bad luck to eavesdrop on a vocal cow or to spy on the seal-folk when they become human. The seal-folk, or *selkies*, are among the most beloved of all the Folk. Like Orkney, Iceland was settled by a combination of Celts and Vikings, and Icelandic lore combines the lore of both.

New Year's Eve is also the time when the Elves change their houses. There is no taboo against watching the Elves move. In fact, the people of Iceland say that if you wait at the crossroads for the Elves to pass, they will give you gold.

In Iceland, water turns to wine on New Year's Eve. If it turns to blood instead, the people believe that their Parliament will be especially contentious that year. Weather predicts the fortunes of the family. If frost collects on the pantry floor on New Year's Eve, the family will have a happy and prosperous year.

In earlier times, one more method of divination was practiced in Iceland on New Year's Eve. If a person wanted to see the face of his or her future spouse, that person should go into a pitch-dark room, and look into a mirror. Three times the figure of a man holding a knife would appear in the mirror.

If the questioner kept watching without fear, he or she would be rewarded with a vision of the future spouse.

Bonfires and fireworks greet the coming of the New Year. As in Mallorca, so far to the south, families stay together until midnight. After midnight, the young people go out to dance away the darkness with each other, and with the Folk, eternally young.

Traditional Holiday Fare

Ham Hocks and Blackeyes

Serves 6-8

1 smoked ham hock
1 pound black-eyed peas
1 onion, finely diced
Water to cover
1 tsp granulated garlic
1 tsp ground black pepper
Salt to taste, if needed

Place ham hock in 3-quart heavy saucepan. Wash black-eyed peas, and check them over to make sure there are no pebbles or bits of dirt present. Add black-eyed peas and onion to pot. Pour water over the peas to cover them to a depth of 2 inches. Cover and bring to a boil over medium heat. When it boils, turn heat to low, and simmer for 1 hour. Add garlic and pepper, and simmer until the peas begin to fall apart, another 30 minutes. Remove ham hock. Pull meat from skin and bone. Discard skin and bone, dice meat, and return it to peas. Taste, and add salt if necessary.

Substitute 1 pound ham or smoked sausage for the ham hock if desired.

Meat may be omitted, if a vegetarian dish is desired.

HOPPIN' JOHN

Classically, Hoppin' John is made by cooking rice with black-eyed peas. The problem with this technique is that black-eyed peas require three times as long to cook to perfection as rice. I prefer to cook the rice separately, and ladle ham hocks and blackeyes over rice on the serving plate.

SMOKED PORK CHOPS AND SAUERKRAUT

Serves 6-8

2 pounds smoked pork chops
1 quart good-quality commercial sauerkraut
2 apples, thinly sliced
1 onion, thinly sliced

Brown pork chops in large, nonreactive skillet. Drain sauerkraut, and rinse with cold water. Layer sauerkraut, apples, and onions over pork chops. Cover and simmer over low heat for 40 minutes.

Serve with noodles or boiled potatoes.

CHAPTER 2
THREE KINGS' DAY
EPIPHANY
January 6

In January, the northern hemisphere still has to look forward to the worst of its winter weather. In hope of spring to come, the winter festivals end now, and the spring festivals begin. January 6, known in medieval England as Twelfth Night, is ignored by most Anglo-Americans. In Europe, Latin America, and one corner of the U.S., it is celebrated in high style.

In most Catholic counties, Three Kings' Day is the formal end of the Christmas season. Children go back to school the next day, and their parents go back to work. This is the last chance for a Christmas party, and they take that chance.

In Germany, people go caroling door to door. The Christmas tree, which was put up on Christmas Eve, is taken down on January 6. This is a festive event for the children, as they will finally be allowed to eat the candy and cookies that have adorned the tree. To share the bounty with the birds and the Folk, take the tree outside, with the cookies and popcorn chains still on it.

In the old days, communities collected the discarded trees on this day, and used them to fuel a public bonfire. Bonfires always attract fire spirits, such as peries and salamanders. People throw parties to use up the last of the Christmas goodies, and sing Christmas carols for the last time until next winter. The Three Kings' Cake makes its appearance, a close cousin of the King Cake that Americans know from Mardi Gras.

In Mexico, Puerto Rico, and most other Latin American locales, children leave boxes of grass under their beds on the night before Epiphany. This is a treat for the Three Kings' camels. The original Kings and their camels, of course, have been gone for many hundreds of years. The Kings who continue to make their rounds in tropical countries are of supernatural origin. In the morning, the grass will be gone, which is proof that the Kings have come. In place of the grass are sweets and toys. Families and friends exchange gifts. As in Germany, they serve a special cake in honor of the Three Kings. As in New Orleans, whoever finds the token in the cake, which may be a bean, a nut, or a tiny doll, is obligated to throw a party on February 2, Candelaria. Finally, they take the decorations down, and Christmas officially ends.

As Mallorca is an island, it differs slightly from other Spanish-influenced areas in its celebration of Three Kings' Day. The Three Kings arrive on the island by boat on January 5. A parade takes them from the dock to the town. Children must go to bed early, so the Kings can leave their presents under their beds while they sleep.

In Ireland, January 6 is known as "Little Christmas." It is the last day on which it is proper to throw Christmas parties.

In Iceland, the Elves dance. As in the British Isles, the northern lights are seen as the visible manifestation of the presence of the Folk. People also have bonfires. Yes, they just had bonfires on New Year's Eve. As cold and dark as Iceland is at midwinter, its inhabitants take every opportunity to warm and brighten it with bonfires.

In Canada, January 6 is one of the dates on which some communities celebrate the Feast of Fools. Other communities celebrate it on December 25, as was done in medieval France, or on January 1. Social customs are upended on the Feast of Fools. Chaos reigns. The Folk walk and dance among us.

And, of course, Epiphany marks the beginning of the Mardi Gras season in New Orleans.

TRADITIONAL HOLIDAY FARE

ROSCA DE LOS REYES: MEXICAN THREE KINGS' CAKE

Serves 16

½ cup warm milk
1 packet active dry yeast
½ cup granulated sugar
2 cups flour
½ cup butter, room temperature
Grated rind of 1 orange
Grated rind of 1 lemon
¼ tsp salt
2 whole eggs, beaten with 3 extra egg yolks
1 ½ cups total, any combination of dried and candied fruits

Soften yeast in milk. In a large mixing bowl, beat together all ingredients except the fruit, until well blended. Stir in the fruit. Turn into a well-greased bundt pan, cover, and let rise in warm place until doubled in volume, 1 hour or more.

Bake at 375º for 30 minutes, or until golden and springy to the touch. Cool in pan for 10 minutes, then invert onto wire rack to cool completely.

Glaze

1 ½ cup confectioners' sugar
2 Tbsp milk
½ tsp vanilla extract

Whisk all ingredients together until smooth. Pour evenly over cooled cake.

CHAPTER 3
GROUNDHOG DAY
CANDLEMAS
IMBOLC
February 2

On February 1, Ireland celebrates St. Brigid's Day. Prior to the Christianization of Ireland, Brigid was the goddess of poetry, healing, and metalwork. The Church, knowing that it could never erase the love of Brigid from the Irish heart, named her a saint, but her character has remained unchanged—as have the rites performed in her honor. As St. Brigid, she remains the patroness of poetry, healing, and metalwork. In the folk imagination, she is also a queen among the Fair Ones.

In her honor, on this day, people weave equal-armed crosses of straw. These "Brigid's Crosses," as they are called, then hang in the kitchen as a blessing on the food, and over doorways, to prevent fire and evil influences from entering. Young women parade through the streets, carrying armfuls of green rushes.

In Orkney, boys reenact a legend about trolls. The older boys dress as old women, and hide. The younger boys, carrying torches, seek out the older ones. When they find them, the tables turn. The older boys chase the younger ones through the streets.

In mainstream America, people gather around water coolers and debate whether the groundhog seeing his shadow means an early spring or a late one. We remember that it has something to do with the weather, but we are not quite sure what. In fact, the old belief is that a sunny day on February 2, allowing the groundhog to see his shadow, presages a long winter. When Roman legions conquered much of Europe, they brought with them the notion of predicting the weather by means of animal behavior. Then, the prescient animal was the hedgehog. Lacking hedgehogs in America, the Pennsylvania Dutch (actually *Deutsch*, or German) transferred the practice to groundhogs.

American Neopagans celebrate February 2 enthusiastically, calling it Imbolc. They believe that the Fair Folk come indoors on the evening of the first. For the comfort of the Folk, Neopagans leave food for them, buttered bread and cakes. Whatever remains on the second, they take outside. They also set out trays of freshly sprouted grass, as a token of spring soon to come. Nurseries sell flats of grass ready to use, or you can sprout your own easily.

To sprout grass:

Spread a layer of gravel in a shallow bowl. Add commercial potting soil to within an inch of the top. Scatter grass seed on top of this, as thickly as salt on a pretzel. Add just a touch more soil, less than $\frac{1}{16}$ of an inch. Press it all down gently with your hand, just enough so that you know the seeds are touching the soil. Water daily with a spray bottle. As there is no drainage, be careful not to overwater.

If you do this at Epiphany, the trays of grass will be ready for Imbolc. If you start a new tray every month or so, you will be able to keep fresh greenery in the house until genuine spring makes it unnecessary. The trays of grass provide a comfortable resting place for any house-elves who may be in residence, as well as for any wood-elves who have come indoors for the winter.

However wintry the weather may be, Imbolc is the time to prepare for spring. Clean and repair your fishing gear, your sporting equipment, your gardening tools (if you did not do so before putting them away in the fall). This shows faith that spring will indeed win out over winter.

Light candles. Tell stories. If any part of the Christmas tree is still in the house, burn it as a sign that winter is no longer welcome.

Feast on dairy products. This is the time for cheesecake, for Welsh Rabbit. Imbolc celebrates the return of fresh milk after a dry winter. The Fair Folk like butterfat, so on this one day, splurge. Imbolc comes but once a year.

TRADITIONAL HOLIDAY FARE

OSTKAKA:
SWEDISH CHEESECAKE

Serves 9 for dessert, 6 for breakfast

The nineteenth-century recipe I found called for a gallon of whole milk, and took over 24 hours to prepare. After spending 18 hours on the first step and 6 hours on the second, I found that I had made (drumroll, please): a quart of cottage cheese.

Making the cottage cheese would have made sense to the residents of isolated farms. They would have had fresh milk every day, and no ready grocery store. Since I get my milk from the same market as my cottage cheese, I hereby give directions with a slight head start.

1 quart cottage cheese
1 cup heavy cream
¾ cup flour
¾ cup granulated sugar
3 eggs

Preheat oven to 400°. Beat together all ingredients until well blended. Turn into greased 8-inch by 8-inch glass baking pan. Bake at 400° for 1 hour. Reduce heat to 300°, and bake for another 25 minutes. Remove from oven, and let rest for 30 minutes before serving.

This is traditionally served with lingonberries or raspberry jam, as a dessert. It is also good without embellishment, for breakfast.

CHAPTER 4
VALENTINE'S DAY
LUPERCALIA
February 14

I n Japan, February 14 is the day on which women give chocolates to men. Don't worry—the men will reciprocate in kind later.

In Finland, February 14 is Friendship Day. Friends exchange cards and small gifts, without reference to romantic entanglements.

The big story is the evolution of Lupercalia into the Valentine's Day we know in the West. In ancient Rome, Lupercalia, February 14, was the festival in honor of the goddess of feverish love. So that no one would be without a partner for this festival, men drew the names of women by lot. How the relationship developed after the lottery was the business of the participants only. The couples might be together for a few days, or a few months. In some cases, they might fall in love and live happily ever after.

When the Roman Empire adopted Christianity, the Church found this festival unacceptable. The lottery was not even limited to unmarried people, but was open to every adult who wanted to participate! The church was powerless to stop the lottery, but expended great effort to change its meaning. First, they had men draw the names of saints by lot. The object was for the men to emulate the virtues of the saint for a year. This proved less popular than drawing the name of a new girlfriend.

Men returned to the process of drawing the names of women. Under pressure from the Church, the assumption of sexual license was discarded, and the pairings became more courtly in nature. The men and women would exchange gifts and compliments, but little more. This continued into the eighteenth century. At that time, the custom became that the gentlemen would buy expensive gifts for the ladies, who were not expected to reciprocate. Giving expensive gifts to women with whom they were not in love or sexually involved, and who did not return the favor, proved fatally unpopular with the men, who put a hasty stop to the practice. Since then, men and women choose each other according to their tastes, rather than by lot.

There are several ways to get the Folk to reveal, on Valentine's Day, the identity of one's future mate. The first is to pin bay leaves to one's pillow before retiring on February 13. Doing this will bring dreams of the future spouse.

The next several methods relate to the old belief that birds choose their mates on St. Valentine's Day. A girl's observations of birds on this day reveal her future husband. If she sees a robin flying overhead , she will marry a sailor. If she sees a sparrow, she will marry a poor man, but they will be happy. If she sees a goldfinch, she will marry a rich man. I wonder if British mothers keep goldfinches handy, for their daughters' benefit?

There are two other ways to get the Folk to reveal a girl's future, which use apples as the source of revelation. A young woman can cut an apple open and count the seeds. The number of seeds she finds is the number of children she will bear. To find out whom she will marry, a girl can recite the names of all her potential suitors, while twisting the stem of the apple. The one whose name she is speaking when the stem breaks is the one she will marry.

What does St. Valentine have to do with any of this? There were two, possibly three, saints named Valentine, whose stories have become confused. The clearest story is that Emperor Claudius the Cruel reasoned that family men made poor soldiers. Family men are more concerned with taking care of their wives and children than with expanding the Empire. For this reason, he banned marriage. Valentine continued to perform marriage ceremonies in secret, in violation of Claudius's edict. Valentine was imprisoned, and executed on February 14. For honoring love above his own safety, he became the patron saint of lovers. The Folk endorse love matches. They watch to see how events unfold, and sometimes work to ease love's path.

For people already coupled, Valentine's Day calls for a party for two. An intimate dinner, preferably at home, is de rigueur. Decorate the room with red roses, emblematic of passion. Serve extravagant foods. Choose dishes with aphrodisiac properties, or erotic connotations. Oysters, lobster, and steak are appropriate entrees. Chocolate, known as an aphrodisiac since Aztec times, is the best choice for a dessert. Dress for maximum visual appeal. Depending on the couple involved, this may mean evening wear, or it may mean night wear. An early bedtime is expected.

The Fair Folk find much amusement in such goings on.

Those who are not already coupled need not sit home and sulk on Valentine's Day. An unattached person can throw a party for other unattached people. If each person brings a single friend or relative of the opposite sex, the numbers will work out evenly, and the chances of meeting someone compatible will be greatly enhanced. You never know whom you might meet.

Traditional Holiday Fare

Truffles

Makes slightly over 1 pound

It is easy to make better truffles than you can buy. Just start with good chocolate, and let your imagination run free.

1 pound best-quality bittersweet chocolate

¾ cup heavy cream

1 tsp any flavoring extract or 3 Tbsp liqueur of choice

½ cup cocoa powder

Chop chocolate, and place in heat-proof mixing bowl. Bring cream to boiling point. Pour boiling cream over chopped chocolate. Stir until melted and smooth. Stir in flavoring. Place in refrigerator until firm enough to shape easily, about 1 hour. Shape into balls by hand. Roll in cocoa and chill until firm. Store in an airtight package in the refrigerator.

CHAPTER 5
CARNIVAL
January 6 until Mardi Gras

Carnival is an international celebration with many meanings and many purposes. The dates and the words describing the practices of Carnival come from the Catholic Church, but the festival itself predates the Church. In central Europe, Carnival began as a fertility rite, a means of driving off the last vestiges of winter, and a celebration of faith that winter will indeed end. The wearing of masks, the role playing, and the feasting are ancient customs.

Some of the practices now associated with Carnival were previously part of Yule, the celebration of the winter solstice. The Kings of the Krewes-the various Mardi Gras associations responsible for putting on parades and balls in Louisiana-are analogous to the King of Fools, a poor outcast who reigned unquestioned over the Feast of Fools. The Feast of Fools was an outgrowth of Saturnalia, and took place on or near the winter solstice. During the Feast of Fools, masters waited on their servants, and slaves ruled over their masters. Men dressed in women's clothing. All was dancing and fun. On Mardi Gras in New Orleans, the King of at least one Krewe occupies City Hall, driving out the elected mayor. Other Carnival practices, still widely celebrated, are drawn from Lupercalia, mentioned in the previous chapter. These include public nudity and sexual abandon.

The duration of Carnival varies from year to year. The beginning of the season is always January 6, but the climax, Mardi Gras, varies according to the date of Easter. If you want to figure it out yourself, Easter is the first Sunday after the first full moon after the vernal equinox. Mardi Gras is forty-one days before that. More simply, just look it up. The date is on most American calendars. If Mardi Gras is not listed in its own right, it is the day before Ash Wednesday. No matter how the phases of the moon fall in relation to the days of the week and the progress of the solar year, Mardi Gras will always fall somewhere between mid-February and mid-March.

Authorities disagree about the meaning of the word "Carnival." Most say that it means "Farewell to meat," and refers to the old practice of abstaining completely from animal foods for the duration of Lent. A few disagree. They maintain that "Carnival" derives from Carrus Navalis, "wagon-ship," referring to the Ship of Fools. According to this argument, the Ship of Fools was a wheeled boat that was pulled through towns for the amusement of the populace. It carried people wearing masks, throwing sweets and baubles to onlookers. A more accurate description of a modern Mardi Gras parade would be hard to come by, but the parades described took place thousands of years ago, in honor of ancient gods.

While the modern rationalization for Carnival was as a preparation for the deprivations of Lent, by the nineteenth century it had spread into Protestant areas. Why miss a party, just because there is nothing to give up afterward?

From Germany to Brazil, from England to New Orleans, Carnival is a grand celebration of noise, costumes, parades, and games. Masks fulfill various purposes. They enable the celebrants to assume grandiose personae, and to avoid future repercussions for misbehavior. There is protection in anonymity. A third purpose, related to the safety of anonymity, is to allow supernatural beings to mingle with human beings. That masked stranger may not be the college student from Des Moines, as he pretends.

A few specific, regional customs deserve mention. In England, women run races while flipping pancakes. The pancakes represent the rich food they will have to do without for the next several weeks. In Mexico, the day before Mardi Gras is called "The Day of the Oppressed Husband." On this day, married men are free to do whatever they like, within the law. Freedom from conventional taboos is an attribute of the Folk, so they approve this custom. In Germany, the Thursday before Mardi Gras is "Women's Carnival." Women roam the streets with scissors, cutting the ties off any men brave, or forgetful, enough to be wearing them. Like Bacchantes, they are devoted to revelry above order. As they are participating in the rites of gods and demigods, ecstasy and lawlessness are religious obligations.

In New Orleans, there are parades every day from Epiphany until Mardi Gras itself. The Three Kings Cake, which is part of the Epiphany celebrations in every Catholic country, becomes the King Cake in New Orleans, available for the duration of the season.

While custom demands that revelry stop at the stroke of midnight on Mardi Gras, it is hard to stop that much party momentum. On Bourbon Street, the debauchery continues until the college kids go back to school. This can take another week or two. On the first Sunday in Lent, Germans light great bonfires. They say that they are burning the spirit of Carnival, but when is a bonfire not a festive occasion in itself? Even in pious Ireland, the first Sunday in Lent is devoted to teasing unmarried adults about their lack of sexual activity.

When people wear masks, the Folk are free to mingle among us. When people are drinking and dancing and behaving in ways that are out of the ordinary, the Folk enjoy joining in.

TRADITIONAL HOLIDAY FARE

JAMBALAYA

Serves 8

2 cups rice

1 tsp salt

4 cups water

2 Tbsp oil

1 pound boneless, skinless chicken breast, diced

½ bunch celery, diced

1 large onion, diced

2 green peppers, diced

1 large ripe tomato, diced

1 small can tomato paste

1 tsp granulated garlic

2 bay leaves

½ tsp thyme

½ tsp red pepper

1 Tbsp Worcestershire sauce

1 pound smoked sausage, sliced

2 pounds cooked ham, diced

Place rice, salt, and water in saucepan. Cover, bring to boil over high heat, turn heat to low, and steam for 20 minutes.

Heat oil in large, nonreactive skillet. Sauté chicken until it turns white. Add celery, onion, and peppers, and continue to sauté until vegetables become tender. Add remainder of ingredients and simmer for 20 minutes. Mix in cooked rice, add salt if needed, and serve.

CHAPTER 6
ST. PATRICK'S DAY
March 17

S
t. Patrick's Day is another spring festival with echoes of the fairy faith, held near the vernal equinox. Everyone is expected to wear green on this date, whether or not they trace their ancestry to Ireland. Anyone who wishes may pinch those who do not wear green. While the pinches will generally be delivered by schoolchildren, pinching is the traditional punishment meted out by the Folk for minor transgressions. Green is also the traditional fairy color, among the Celts.

What started out as an ethnic festival has long since crossed over barriers of heritage, to include anyone who wishes to party. Formal balls are held on St. Patrick's Day from Rome to Malaysia. The Sidhe, who include royalty and former gods among their number, are welcome to participate in these. In Russia, St. Patrick's Day is combined with a Russian Carnival celebration, the Maslinitsa. In proper hybrid fashion, performances of Russian folk dances are rewarded with mugs of Irish beer. This kind of festival is more congenial than formal balls to the hardworking Folk common among the Celts. After a year of tending livestock, encouraging the growth of crops, and making handicrafts, the Folk want to let their hair down.

In Florence, Italy, they celebrate a ten-day-long Irish festival, serving Italian interpretations of such Irish dishes as potato soup, boiled beef, and smoked salmon.

In Japan, kilted bands of Japanese bagpipers march in a parade, led by the Irish ambassador. "Voucher girls" hand out coupons, redeemable for free beer at the local bars. The mind boggles.

In Australia, where much of the population boasts Irish descent, the whole month of March is set aside for partying. They have not just parades and parties, but horse races, golf tournaments, and concerts. Never before has the humble leprechaun been entertained so grandly.

Parades are held not just in New York and Boston, but in Seattle, Toronto, and Oslo, Norway. For some reason not clear to me, the St. Patrick's Day parade in Manchester, England, features samba bands. Perhaps the upright and precise movements of Irish folk dancing are not sensual enough for the Folk at a spring festival, a celebration of fertility.

Many assert that St. Patrick's Day is primarily an American festival, and no big deal in Ireland. Perhaps, a generation ago, an Irish St. Patrick's Day may have warranted only a trip to church and a couple of pints in the local pub, but that has changed. The parade held in Dublin nowadays matches the extravagance and enthusiasm of Mardi Gras in New Orleans.

The usual entrée on St. Patrick's Day in the U.S., boiled corned beef, is unknown in Ireland. There, the meal would center on ham or Irish bacon, a cured pork loin similar to Canadian bacon. There is a reason for this anomaly. When the Irish migrated to the States in the 1840s to escape the famine, they were shunted into neighborhoods that were primarily Jewish. The kosher butchers in these neighborhoods did not carry ham or bacon, so the Irish immigrants switched to the cured meat product they could obtain: corned beef. What began as an improvised substitution has become a rock-solid tradition itself. What Irish-American would invite a leprechaun to sit down to any other dinner on St. Patrick's Day than corned beef?

TRADITIONAL HOLIDAY FARE

NEW ENGLAND BOILED DINNER

Serves 4

My father's family left Ireland during the Hunger, and reached California only after a couple of generations in Boston. This is the way my father taught me to cook for St. Patrick's Day.

4 pounds corned beef brisket

Water to cover

4 large or 8 medium potatoes, unpeeled

6 large carrots, peeled and cut into 2-inch lengths

4 onions, peeled and cut into quarters

1 head white cabbage, cut into eighths

Three hours before dinnertime, cover corned beef with cold water in a large saucepan. Bring to a simmer, and cook for two hours. Add vegetables, and simmer for 1 hour more. Serve with butter for the vegetables and mustard for the meat.

If your tastes were formed at any time in the last four decades, you will recognize that the vegetables are terminally overcooked by this method. If you would like your taste of "Kiss me I'm Irish" patriotism less dated, try:

CORNED BEEF AND CABBAGE REDUX

Serves 4

4 pounds corned beef brisket

Water to cover

2 Tbsp butter

2 onions, coarsely chopped

1 head white cabbage, coarsely chopped

Simmer brisket for 3 hours, as above. Twenty minutes before mealtime, heat a large skillet. Saute onions in butter until soft. Add cabbage, toss to mix, cover, and steam over low heat for 10 minutes, or until done to your taste. Serve with mashed potatoes and raw baby carrots.

CHAPTER 7
ST. JOSEPH'S DAY
March 19

New Orleans's heritage is a complex blend of French, Spanish, African, and American customs, so no one should be surprised that this city celebrates the holidays in ways seen nowhere else in America. One holiday so celebrated is St. Joseph's Day, near the vernal equinox.

The custom in New Orleans on St. Joseph's Day is to build huge altars, and decorate them with all the finery at hand: bridal veils, Christmas tree ornaments, fresh flowers, and potted plants. On the altar, the hosts will place hundreds of different kinds of food.

The feast begins with a man representing St. Joseph, a little girl representing Mary, and as many orphans as the hosts can persuade to join them. The people of New Orleans consider it lucky to feed orphans on St. Joseph's Day. Having no earthly family ties, orphans are regarded as belonging to the Folk. After these principals have eaten their fill, the hosts open the altar to the entire community. If the host family is requesting a boon, the guests form a procession to the neighborhood church. The procession itself is a magical ceremony designed to coerce the Powers, be they God or the Folk, to grant the hosts' desire. They are careful not to trip or stub their toes, for to do so would be unlucky. They also take care to return to the host's home by the exact route they took to the church, for the same reason. Such precision is typical of rituals requesting favors of the Folk.

All the leftover food is given to the poor. In some cases, the entire altar is given to an orphanage. In these cases, the orphanage keeps the food for the use of its residents, who are under the patronage of the Folk. The people celebrating St. Joseph's Day are currying favor with the Folk by showing kindness to their dependants.

Whether the altar is in a home or an institution, the hosts distribute bread and beans. The guests keep these all year. The bread protects the families of the guests from starvation, and the beans bring luck. In fact, some altars are supported by professional gamblers, who rely on the beans for their livelihoods.

In the twentieth century, the custom of having massive public feasts on St. Joseph's Day spread beyond the Italian Catholic community of New Orleans. By mid-century, the people there celebrated St. Joseph's Day irrespective of religion or ethnicity. All celebrants expect good luck to follow their participation in the feasts, whether they are involved as hosts or as guests.

While on the surface St. Joseph's Day is a Catholic festival, on a deeper level it is a rite designed to strengthen the ties between the human community and the Folk. The charitable feasts and ritual processions are magic spells to obtain favors from the spirit realm, which is indistinguishable from Faerie.

Entertaining strangers is a common motif in interactions between human beings and the Folk.

More evidence that the St. Joseph's Day traditions predate and underlie Catholic practices is that the Catholic Church has been unsuccessful in suppressing them when they have conflicted with other Catholic obligations.

Incidentally, St. Joseph's Day is the date on which the swallows come back to Capistrano. They arrive all together, on one day, as if by magic. No one living more than fifty miles from Capistrano would know this, were it not for a sentimental song written by Leon Rene, who was from New Orleans.

TRADITIONAL HOLIDAY FARE

The array of food on the typical St. Joseph's Day altar is so vast that no one dish exemplifies it. Any food that is Italian, French, Spanish, African, Irish, or Caribbean in derivation is appropriate.

CHAPTER 8
VERNAL EQUINOX
Approximately March 21

So many spring festivals have moved around, due to changes in the calendar, that few celebrations remain attached to the equinox itself. Mad revelry goes on at Carnival and on St. Patrick's Day. Easter and Mother's Day are occasions for reverence. On March 21 itself, little goes on.

In Germany 1,500 years ago, the vernal equinox was seen as the rebirth of Nature, the resurrection of the sun god, and the beginning of the New Year, but it is no longer celebrated. The spring rites have moved to Easter and May Day.

When Persia was Persia, before it became Iran, the spring equinox was the New Year. Business stopped for thirteen days. Rich and poor alike picnicked in the countryside, in honor of spring.

In Sweden, the equinox is Lady Day, and is a celebration of Mother Nature. The Swedish word for "Lady Day" sounds like "Waffle Day," so they celebrate by feasting on heart-shaped waffles. It is a coincidence that many Americans serve waffles to their wives and mothers on Mother's Day. Changes in the calendar have moved the date of the celebration away from the solar event it marks; Lady Day is celebrated on March 25.

The Japanese visit family graves on the vernal equinox. Their spring celebration depends on visible signs of spring. Once the cherry trees bloom, they will picnic among the blossoms. The Fair Folk are famous admirers of flowering fruit trees, in Japan as in the rest of the world. Sharing an outdoor meal in the shade of a blooming orchard is a sure method of consorting with the Folk.

When Americans choose to celebrate the vernal equinox as a holiday in its own right, the rites are the same as for Easter or May Day. Because the vernal equinox commemorates the reunion of Demeter and Persephone, mothers and daughters should be especially kind to one another. Demeter is the goddess of orchards and fields of grain. Persephone, her daughter, is the goddess of youth and spring. Only when they are together can crops grow. Their separation causes winter.

One theme I have found in my researches, over and over, is that of cleaning house thoroughly, in advance of holidays. The Folk despise slovenliness, and punish it with pinching and poverty. Conversely, they reward neatness with good health, happiness, and prosperity. The idea of spring cleaning is still current in our language, even though we tend to maintain the same standard of cleanliness all year, nowadays. Every culture I have studied has at least one time each year when everyone is expected to pitch in and make the home immaculate. When cleaning for ritual purposes, to gain the favor of the Folk, you should scrub in a clockwise direction. Whether this will build up positive energy in the home I cannot tell, but it will keep your mind focused on the spiritual value of cleaning. Intention is everything.

Clean and rededicate outdoor shrines every spring. Leave out offerings of hard boiled eggs, honey cakes, and milk punch, for the Folk.

TRADITIONAL HOLIDAY FARE

GINGER HONEYCAKES

Makes 3 dozen

¾ cup butter
2 cups granulated sugar
2 eggs
1 Tbsp vinegar
½ cup honey
3 ¾ cups all-purpose flour
1 ½ tsp baking soda
4 tsp ground ginger
½ tsp ground cinnamon
¼ tsp ground cloves
¼ cup candied ginger, finely chopped
Additional sugar for decoration

Cream butter and sugar together until fluffy. Beat in eggs, vinegar, and honey until thoroughly blended.

In a separate bowl, stir together the dry ingredients. Toss chopped candied ginger with dry ingredients. Add flour mixture to butter mixture, and stir until a smooth dough forms.

Shape dough into walnut-sized ball, dip in sugar, and place 2 inches apart on cookie sheets treated with nonstick spray. Bake at 350° for 12 minutes, or until evenly golden.

CHAPTER 9
APRIL FOOLS' DAY
April 1

hroughout Europe and North America, people celebrate April Fools' Day by playing practical jokes on one another. Some believe that doing so is symbolic of the changeable nature of the weather in April. Others assert that it is the remnant of changes made to the calendar in the Middle Ages. In either case, April Fools' Day has been celebrated since the sixteenth century. It is the day on which human beings are as free to indulge in pranks as the Folk are all year.

In France and Belgium, the game of the day is "April Fish." People surreptitiously pin a fish on the back of someone else's clothing. In France, this is usually a cut-out paper fish. In Belgium, it may well be a real fish. When the victim of the prank discovers the fish, the perpetrator yells, "April Fish!"

In Newfoundland, the custom is to tell outrageous lies all morning. Many stories are even reported on respected television and radio news shows. At noon, the liars confess, and congratulate themselves for their cleverness.

In Orkney, the gags go on for three days. People play the usual assortment of pranks on the first of the month. On the second, they pin tails on each other. On the third, anything they borrow magically becomes their property, and need never be returned.

All of these customs echo the behavior of the Folk, when they are in their mischievous mode. Many old stories tell of this aspect of the folk. In one, a man forced a leprechaun to reveal the location of his buried gold. Having no shovel with him, the man tied a ribbon to a blade of grass to mark the location of the gold. When he returned with a shovel a few minutes later, he found that there was a ribbon tied to every blade of grass in the field. April Fool!

For an April Fool party, arrange competitions for the best tall tale, and the best harmless practical joke. Food can be made in odd colors or deceptive shapes, but use restraint. No one will touch the cake made to look like a used cat box, no matter how much they trust the cook.

Don't ask me how I know this.

TRADITIONAL HOLIDAY FARE

"POACHED EGGS"

Serves 8

1 medium can apricot halves, drained (approximately 18
    ounces)
2 envelopes unflavored gelatin
½ cup water
3 ½ cups milk
¾ cup granulated sugar
1 tsp almond extract

Place 1 apricot half in each of eight small dessert bowls, round side up. Set aside.

Sprinkle gelatin over water, and allow to sit at room temperature while scalding milk and sugar over medium-low heat. When bubbles form around edges of milk mixture, pour gelatin mixture into it. Remove from heat and stir until gelatin is completely melted. Stir in almond extract.

Pour ½ cup gelatin mixture over each apricot half, and chill until firm.

CHAPTER 10
EASTER
Date varies

Easter is an ancient holiday that is still celebrated under its original name, with many of its original symbols intact.

Easter, Eostre, Ostara, Astarte, and Isis are all names for the Great Goddess. She is Mother of the world, bringer of fertility and abundance. Her symbols are the hare and the egg, also widely associated with abundance, fertility, and springtime.

An old legend states that Eostre saved the life of a bird whose wings had caught fire, by turning her into a hare. The transformation into a hare was incomplete, however, as she still laid eggs in the manner of a bird. Whether this is the origin of the Easter bunny, I cannot say. The story may have been made up after the fact, to explain the presence of an egg-bringing hare in the popular imagination. Composite animals are among the denizens of Faerie.

By the way, rabbits and hares are not the same animal. Rabbits are naked and helpless when born, while hares are born with fur, and able to hop around. As they are commonly confused in the minds of the people, they are usually interchangeable as symbols.

In addition to being a well-known symbol of fecundity, the hare is emblematic of the moon, which is, in turn, connected to the Goddess. Some cultures, such as the Chinese, see a hare in the pattern of light and dark on the lunar surface, not a man. To this day, the date of Easter each year is determined by the phases of the moon. As stated earlier, Easter is the first Sunday after the first full moon after the vernal equinox.

The egg, as well as being an obvious symbol of fertility, is also a symbol of beauty, order, harmony, and perfection. Who has never admired the shape and texture of an eggshell? In the egg is the future bird, so the egg becomes as well a symbol of hope and potential. It is, in microcosm, the Cosmic Egg, the Universe itself. The egg is an object of fascination and reverence among the Folk, as it is among human beings.

The newly hatched chicks we honor at Easter were no throwaway playthings in agricultural societies. The fluffy chicks would become the laying hens that would provide high-quality protein later, and perhaps some spending money as well. The chicks were valued, not for their looks alone, but for their contribution to the family's well-being. The Folk abhor waste, especially the waste of life. Give chicks as Easter gifts only if you maintain a henhouse.

If you have not already cleaned house for one of the other spring festivals, do it prior to Easter. Decorate with flowers and baskets of grass. The Russians, who take Easter seriously, originated the custom of sprouting grass indoors for Easter decorations. They also dye eggs by boiling them with onion skins or red cabbage. Onion skins give subtle tan shades to white eggs. Red cabbage dyes them a brilliant blue. On Easter morning, they put the eggs into nests their children have made, on the previous day, near the front door. While the Easter Bunny gets the credit for bringing the eggs, it is the child's parents who provide the blessings. We each have a fairy-nature as part of our being. Love is part of that fairy-nature.

Easter trees, decorated with eggs, are a recent phenomenon in the U.S., but an old one in Germany. There is no need to spend a fortune on expensive glass ornaments. Blow out real eggs, and decorate them by hand. The results will be just as beautiful, and much more satisfying to the soul. The Folk have no affinity for mass-produced objects, but are attracted to the handmade crafts.

The early English settlers in America avoided celebrating Easter. They found the cheerful Paganism of eggs and bunnies un-Christian. For this reason, most of the Easter traditions we consider American have German, rather than English, roots. Some of the German customs that Americans have taken into their hearts include a religious service at sunrise, a big family brunch, Easter egg hunts for the children, ham for dinner, leftover hard-boiled eggs on the menu for weeks, dyed eggs, and eggs made out of various kinds of candy. The Easter Bunny, in Germany as well as in America, is a nondiscriminatory giver of gifts. He does not care whether a child has been "naughty or nice." Children receive baskets of candy, a small toy or two, and more hard-boiled eggs than they ever wanted. The Easter egg hunt is an ideal time to encourage children to look in the garden, in the shady nooks and secret places where the Folk hide. They will excuse the intrusion on Easter, as Easter is a special day.

There are other German traditions that did not cross the Atlantic successfully. In some locales, people erect a Paschal Pole, like a May Pole, decorated with flowers and ribbons. The Folk are partial to all kinds of floral decorations. People light bonfires on the night before Easter, presumably to protect the settlements while God is away on business. Because bonfires are usually set to repel the Folk, it is best to avoid them if you want the Folk to participate in the egg hunt on Easter. They might take it the wrong way.

On Palm Sunday, groups of girls walk through the towns singing, carrying a ball on a stick. The stick is decorated with flowers and ribbons, as the Paschal Pole would be. People reward them with eggs and sweets. Both the carolers and the ones who give them treats are in favor with the Folk.

There is a bit of traditional Easter love magic practiced in Germany. Before dawn on Easter, young single women go out to bathe in natural springs. If one of these women wants to get married, she brings back some of the spring water and sprinkles her sweetheart with it. A wedding will follow shortly. The Folk will arrange matters, for those who follow their rites.

Other regions have equally festive customs. In Orkney, boys hold plowing competitions, and children dress up as horses. Lithuanians practice egg rolling all year, in order to excel at Easter. In Mexico, people break cascarones over each other's heads. These are blown eggshells, filled with confetti. Laughter and merriment always attract the friendly Folk.

Swedish children dress up as witches on Holy Thursday, and go door to door, begging gifts. Finnish children do likewise, but on Palm Sunday. The Finnish people believe that the tradition originated within their Greek ethnic community, with influences from the neighboring Swedes. Americans aren't the only people to benefit from ethnic diversity! As the Russians do, the Finns decorate their homes with green grass and yellow flowers. The Folk of many lands travel with the people to whom they have grown accustomed, and with their descendants. In a neighborhood with a population of ethnic Russians, following Russian customs will entice the beautiful, green-haired rusalki to attend your party. To invite them specifically, sing and dance near a stream, and throw wreaths of flowers on the water.

The Irish have many customs regarding Easter. They hold dances on Easter, at which cakes are raffled off. The most free-spending gentleman present "takes the cake." They not only clean their houses prior to Easter, but paint them if necessary. As we do, the Irish buy new clothes for Easter. The Folk are amused to find us, not in our accustomed blue jeans, but decked out in hat and gloves.

On Good Friday, Irish custom forbids working outside the home. The Folk in Ireland have coexisted with Catholicism for centuries and respect its traditions. Because Jesus was tortured and killed by being nailed to a wooden cross, any form of woodworking, especially if it involves hammering nails, is considered just plain rude. So Good Friday is when the Irish paint the interiors of their houses. They also observe absolute silence from noon until 3:00 P.M. The evening meal consists of shellfish and seaweed. This meal puts them in harmony with the merfolk and the selkies who live on their coasts.

The Irish believe that a baby born on Good Friday and baptized on Easter will have healing powers. The ability to heal is an old gift of the merfolk. The gift is passed down in family lines, as a reward for saving the life of a mermaid.

Irish butchers band together on Easter to hold a funeral for the herring. After forty days of doing very little business, they are glad to see the end of Lent. Fasting customers are bad for a butcher's business.

Some traditions are best left in the past. Throughout eastern Europe, young men have chased their sweethearts with willow sticks. The Folk lived in the willow. The women involved, far from resenting the treatment, considered it a mark of favor to be gently beaten on Easter. That a young man would chase her at Easter meant that a proposal of marriage would follow quickly. Not a long-forgotten relic of the past, this tradition is remembered fondly by women still living. One recounted that, after the beating, the women were thrown into a stream, or drenched with a bucket of water. The Folk catch the meaning, and send rain. The women involved were identified with the Folk when participating in this rite. Except at a pool party, when everyone present is in high spirits, I would recommend substituting a doll for a woman in this rite. Drenching a doll is just as likely to bring rain, and less likely to bring other repercussions. Hell hath no fury like a woman wet.

TRADITIONAL HOLIDAY FARE

PASHKA:
LOW-FAT VERSION

Serves 4

1 pint cottage cheese
½ cup plain yogurt
¼ cup granulated sugar
½ tsp vanilla extract

Whir cottage cheese and yogurt together in a blender until smooth. Stir in sugar and vanilla. Pour into mold, and chill overnight. Serve with fruit.

PASHKA:
FULL STRENGTH

Serves 4

1 pound cream cheese
¼ pound butter
2 egg yolks
¼ cup granulated sugar
1 tsp vanilla extract

Allow ingredients to come to room temperature. Blend together thoroughly. Mold, chill overnight, and serve with fruit.

CHAPTER II
MAY DAY
May 1

May Day fell out of favor in the U.S. in the last half of the twentieth century, due to politics. On May 1, eastern Europeans celebrated Labor Day. Since all right-thinking, freedom-loving Americans celebrated Labor Day on the first Monday in September, acknowledging May 1 in any way was tantamount to waving a Soviet flag. Now that the Red Menace has passed, it is time to rehabilitate this most festive of days. We owe that much to the Folk, who have been deprived of their rightful celebration for the last half-century.

Although many of our other holiday traditions derive from German customs, the German imagery behind May 1 is unfamiliar to most of us. The emphasis in Germany is not on May Day, but on the night before it, Walpurgisnacht. Directly opposite Halloween on the solar calendar, Walpurgisnacht resembles the Celtic Halloween more than any other holiday.

On Walpurgisnacht, the Folk leave their underground dwellings to dance on the meadows. Locals can point out the mounds where the Folk live; archaeologists describe the same mounds as ancient burial sites. This underlines the cross-cultural identification of the Folk with the souls of the dead. The traditional German belief is that the Folk rule the month of May, and continue to dwell outdoors until well into summer.

German children dress in costumes and play pranks on their neighbors. Typical pranks include putting toothpaste on doorknobs and adorning trees with toilet paper. The story is often told of a friend of a friend who took apart a cart and reassembled it on the owner's roof. What separates this story from similar ones involving fraternity boys and Volkswagens is that it takes place in the nineteenth century, or earlier. A good practical joke never goes stale. The Folk take a professional interest in the antics of practical jokers. Make sure the jokes are harmless, though. The Folk will avenge wrongs done on their watch.

Chocolate bugs are traditionally given to children as a treat on May Day. Who would have thought that gummy worms and spiders have folkloric antecedents? Leave one or two (not chocolate, as it is toxic to some wildlife) in the crook of a tree, for the Folk.

Coming as it did in the middle of the planting season, May Day was welcomed as a respite from the hard work of farming. On the other hand, people planted seedlings and young trees on May Day, "for luck," which sounds like farming to me. Note that planting in May reflects the realities of a cold climate. If your climate is warmer, plant your lucky trees earlier in the year. The cold climate and late spring are reflected in their proverbs. In Germany, they say, "Rain in May brings blessings," while we say, "April showers bring May flowers." The Folk will abide in the trees we plant with holy intentions, and protect the whole garden from malicious influences.

The people choose a May Queen from among the young women. She declares winter defeated, and starts the May Pole dance. If she is both pretty and kind, the Folk will see that all the dancers prosper.

Arranging the May Pole is more complicated than it appears on the surface. If there are only a handful of participants, they will not form a satisfactory ribbon braid. The more dancers who participate, the taller the pole needs to be to allow room for them all to dance. For a community-wide event, erecting the May Pole involves several strong men and horses.

There was also the ever-present threat of the theft of the May Pole to consider. Neighboring towns were always stealing each other's May Poles, and holding them for ransom. The usual ransom was two or three kegs of beer. Did anyone say, "Frat boys"?

If you want to have a May Pole dance, start with a pole at least ten feet tall. If there are more than ten dancers, add another foot of height for each additional two dancers. In other words, you will need a ten-foot pole for ten or fewer dancers, eleven feet for twelve, twelve feet for fourteen dancers, etc.

MAY DAY

Attach ribbons to the top of the pole, equal to the number of dancers. Each ribbon should be one-third longer than the height of the pole.

Ideally, there should be an equal number of males and females who want to dance. They should stand around the pole, boy-girl-boy-girl, each holding a ribbon taut. On cue, the males circle clockwise, and the females counter-clockwise, passing each other's *right* shoulders. They should alternate going over and under the ribbons of the persons they pass. If each male goes over the ribbon of the first female he passes, and under the next, it will all come out even.

If all the dancers hold their ribbons taut, pass right shoulders, and alternate over-under-over-under, they will wrap the pole in a neat braid that symbol-izes order in the universe. It is unlikely that they will succeed on their first attempt. It is worth the time and effort to practice, because, of all seasonal cel-ebrations, this is the favorite of the winged Folk.

Once you and your friends have practiced the May Pole dance and become proficient, you may want to refine it further. When setting up the pole and ribbons, put a wreath of flowers at the top. Do not fasten it, but let the taut ribbons hold it up. As the dancers form the braid around the pole, the wreath will slowly fall down the pole, until it rests on the ground. The Folk like this version of the dance especially, as it enacts the union of opposites-heaven and earth, spirit and nature, male and female.

Noise is another important part of the celebration of May Day. Not all of the Folk who roam abroad at this time of year are friendly. Loud noises serve to frighten off the unfriendly ones. In parts of Germany, boys climb manure piles and crack whips from their tops. The locals see this as a ritual to ensure the fertility of their fields, but it is just as much an excuse to get exception-ally smelly and dirty. On the Isle of Man, people from all over the island gather to stage a mock battle that lasts until sundown. After sundown, they feast and dance and visit with their friends long into the night. Not all of these friends are mortal.

Also on the Isle of Man, witches were in power on May Day. On May Eve, boys put crosses of rowan wood in their caps, to prevent witches or the Folk from kidnapping them. Remember that rowan is itself a fairy tree, and only witches would know how to protect against fairy abductions. These customs tell only half the story, however, by suggesting that witches and the Folk are forces to be avoided. As with anyone, there are good and bad among them.

On Man, people put potted plants outside their doors and windows, as decoys to prevent the Folk from entering. Of course, one could welcome the Folk by putting the plants *inside* the home. In either case, leave water outside, for the use of the Folk at night. The Manx also set fire to their hedges on May Eve, to create walls of fire. These serve to keep evil influences out of their lands for the entire year, and simultaneously rejuvenate the hedges. I cannot recommend this procedure, however, because of the ever-present danger of wildfire. It is safer to rejuvenate a hedge by pruning it severely. Keep evil influences away by staying on cordial terms with the supernatural beings already in residence.

In Cornwall, women wash their faces with the dew gathered on May Day, to improve their complexions. Early dew, gathered before dawn, carries fairy magic.

In England, the Queen of the May is Maid Marian, and the King of the May is Robin Hood. These two are, and have always been, among the Gentle Folk. Stories confusing them with historical characters came later. Naturally, the English stage archery tournaments. Young people once went into the woods on May Eve, to gather flowers and greenery to decorate their homes. This was a ruse to allow free expression of love, always favored by the Folk. The practice of young people going into the woods unchaperoned, and staying out all night, led to the outlawing of May Day when the Puritans came into power in 1644. While the holiday was restored later, it never recovered its previous glory.

In some parts of France, if a lonely young man wanted to get married, but did not have a likely partner, he could lie in a field on May Day and pretend to sleep. If a girl wanted to marry him, she could "wake" him with a kiss. If they were then agreeable to each other, they would announce their engagement. As in any rite involving chance, it is important to keep in the good graces of the Folk. They will guide their favorites on a happy path.

In Sweden, the people light bonfires on April 30 to scare away wolves and trolls. They do this even if they live in wolf-free cities, and do not believe in trolls. Valborg, the Swedish May Day, is related to the German Walpurgisnacht. Traditionally, it is the first day on which the livestock are turned out to pasture after spending the winter in the barn. From this comes the concern over wolves. They fuel the fires with branches broken from forest trees by winter storms, so the bonfires double as a means of cleaning up the forest. As much as they want to avoid the trolls, who eat people, Swedes want to attract the *tomte*, to guard their homes and families. It is to entertain the *tomte* that Swedes celebrate Valborg by singing, strolling in the city centers, shooting off fireworks, and drinking.

In Finland, Vappu, also related to Walpurgisnacht, is celebrated with a lemony alcoholic drink called *sima*, and fritters indistinguishable from our American funnel cakes. Finns are determined to celebrate the coming of spring at this time, and will do so even if it is snowing. On May Eve, Finns dress up and go from bar to bar, drinking sparkling wine. The resident Folk join them in their rounds, reveling with them in country-fair spirit.

May 1 brings the national hangover. Those who are strong enough go out to lunch with their families later. Children like to picnic. If it is snowing, they will picnic on the living-room floor. They need to show faith in the spirits of spring, never doubting that winter will end. If the Folk have not yet brought sunshine and fair weather, the people encourage them to do so with this show of faith.

In Orkney as well, people light bonfires on Beltane, May Eve. It is taboo to wear winter boots between Beltane and harvest. Even if it snows, which is common this far north, people must wear summer shoes. To do otherwise would show a lack of confidence in the Folk, who will bring summer.

TRADITIONAL HOLIDAY FARE

SIMA:
HARD LEMONADE

Makes six quarts

3 lemons
1 ¼ cups granulated sugar
6 quarts boiling water
¼ tsp active dry yeast
6 tsp additional granulated sugar
12 raisins

Peel yellow part of lemon peel (zest) off lemons with a vegetable peeler, and set aside. Cut away spongy white part of peel, and discard. Slice lemons thinly, and place in a large, nonreactive bowl with lemon zest and first quantity of sugar. Pour boiling water over the lemon mixture, and allow to cool to lukewarm. Add yeast. Cover and allow to stand at room temperature for 12 hours.

In each of six sterile 1-quart bottles, place 1 tsp sugar and 2 raisins. Pour liquid from bowl through sterilized strainer and funnel into prepared bottles and cap tightly. Let stand for 1–2 days at room temperature. It is ready to drink when the raisins come to the top.

Chill before opening. This drink is slightly alcoholic, and foams like champagne. There is a danger of explosion if you use the wrong kind of bottles, so ask an expert at a brewing-supplies store for advice.

MAY DAY

MAY DAY FRITTERS

Makes 4 plate-sized fritters

2 Tbsp warm water

2 tsp active dry yeast

1 cup warm milk

2 eggs, at room temperature

1 ½ tsp granulated sugar

½ tsp salt

2 cups flour

oil for frying

Confectioners' sugar

Soften yeast in water. Mix eggs and sugar in large mixing bowl. Add yeast mixture, milk, and salt. Add flour ¼ cup at a time, beating well with wire whisk after each addition. When smooth, cover and set in a warm place to rise until double in volume. This will take from 1–3 hours, depending on the temperature of your kitchen and the perkiness of your yeast.

When batter has risen, heat ¼ inch of oil in a large cast-iron skillet. The oil is hot enough when a drop of batter placed in the pan sizzles immediately. For each fritter, ladle 1 cup of batter into a funnel. Use the funnel to draw a lacy pattern in batter on the surface of the hot oil. When lightly browned and cooked through, carefully turn with two spatulas. Drain on paper towels, and dust with confectioners' sugar. Repeat until batter is used up.

CHAPTER 12
CINCO DE MAYO
May 5

inco de Mayo, in common with St. Patrick's Day, is an ethnic festival that has transcended ethnic barriers. The whole community comes together for the party.

In Mexico, May 5 is the anniversary of the Battle of Puebla, in 1862. It was not a decisive battle. It was not until later that the French were finally driven out of Mexico. Cinco de Mayo in Mexico is a regional celebration limited to Puebla.

In the United States, however, Cinco de Mayo is a major cultural festival, wherever significant numbers of people boast Mexican descent. Throughout the Southwest, people of all ethnicities gather to eat Mexican food and drink Mexican beer. When I was a cook on a ranch in rural California, Cinco de Mayo was the biggest feast of the year. We brought in extra staff for the whole first week of May, making tamales, various types of chilies and moles, and half a dozen desserts. This went on even though none of the kitchen staff, and few of the residents, had any Mexican forebears.

Where is the connection to the Folk in this? The Folk travel with people, and then cling to the land where their people have once lived. Wherever Southwestern people live, or have lived, there will be Folk who were once the companions of the Native Americans and Spaniards who created the mestizo culture that endures to this day. Dress in brilliant colors, and play Mexican music, to gain the favor of these spirits.

TRADITIONAL HOLIDAY FARE

CHILE VERDE

Serves 4

If you do not want to tell anyone how easy this is to make, I will keep your secret safe.

1 pound cooked pork (see "Roast Pork" in the Yule section)
1 jar salsa verde, approximately 12 ounces

Cut pork into bite-sized pieces. Put into a nonreactive pan. Pour salsa over it. Simmer over low heat for 15 minutes, stirring occasionally. Serve with rice, tortillas, or cornmeal mush.

FLAN ESPECIAL

Serves 6

½ cup sugar
1 fourteen-ounce can sweetened condensed milk
1 twelve-ounce can evaporated milk
4 whole eggs
4 additional egg yolks
1 tsp vanilla extract
½ tsp ground cinnamon
½ tsp ground nutmeg
Grated rind of 1 orange

Preheat oven to 325°. Heat sugar in saucepan on top of stove, stirring frequently, until melted and golden in color. Quickly pour caramelized sugar into pie tin or flan mold, tilting pan quickly to coat bottom.

Beat milks, eggs, yolks, and flavorings together until well combined. Bake at 325° until set, approximately 50 minutes. Cool before serving. To serve, unmold and cut into wedges.

CHAPTER 13
MOTHER'S DAY
Date Varies

In most of the world, a spring day is set aside to honor mothers. This varies, both in the date and the type of celebration. Spring itself is the blessing of Demeter, an outgrowth of her joy at reunion with her daughter, Persephone.

Demeter was the goddess of grain and of the harvest, in ancient Greece. She loved her daughter, Persephone, as every mother loves her daughter. Persephone ran off and married a man of whom her mother did not approve, who happened to be the god of the underworld. In mourning for the loss of her daughter, Demeter ceased to give life to the plants. The world became barren, and people began to starve. Zeus negotiated for Hades to return Persephone to her mother. Before she left the underworld, Persephone ate a few pomegranate seeds, guaranteeing that she would return. Thus she spends each growing season aboveground with her mother, and winter with her husband. Since the gods of abandoned religions transformed into the Folk, Demeter and Persephone are properly honored among them.

In Mexico, Mother's Day is on May 10. Adult children travel to their hometowns on May 9, in order to spend the whole next day with their mothers. Armenia celebrates Mother's Day earlier in the spring, in April. In Greece, it is Rhea, mother of the gods, who is honored. In ancient Rome, the festival of the mother goddess Cybele lasted from March 15 to 18. In England, in an earlier age, the fourth Sunday in Lent was Mothering Sunday. Servants were given the day off to visit their mothers and bring them simnel cakes. In

Finland, Mother's Day is a national holiday, specifically honoring women who have lost their children in military service. Those lost children are highly honored among the Folk, as the North has always reverenced fallen heroes. They should be honored with feasts of roast meat, and toasted with mead.

In the United States, Mother's Day is the second Sunday in May. It is considered a modern and secular holiday, but is observed as strictly as any ancient religious duty. The mothers of small children can reasonably expect breakfast in bed and handmade cards or gifts. In addition, so many families expect to have brunch or dinner in a fine restaurant that it's nearly impossible to do so. In order to avoid crowds, treat Mom as a guest in her own home. Let husband and children prepare Mom's favorite meal from the old family recipes. If that is beyond the family's abilities as cooks, they can certainly pick up and reheat something from the supermarket deli counter. Many large grocery stores nowadays will prepare entire meals to go, with one day's notice. The Folk have high regard for mothers, and pinch children who neglect them.

In some happy cases, whole groups of mothers and their daughters are friends. Mother's Day provides the perfect excuse for a multigenerational tea party. The Folk would be delighted to share the garden with a group of girls and women, sipping tea and eating cake. Be sure to share with them.

TRADITIONAL HOLIDAY FARE

SIMNEL CAKE

Serves 8

A simnel cake, in its classic form, is a spice cake. It is heavy with butter and eggs, studded with raisins and candied cherries, and stuffed and topped with marzipan. While I automatically love anything that involves marzipan, I have changed this cake to better suit American tastes. The candied cherries had to go. They are so closely connected with Yule in the American consciousness, that they are unobtainable in the spring. In addition, not one American in ten will admit to liking fruitcake.

½ pound butter
1 ¼ cups granulated sugar
4 eggs
1 ¾ cups flour
1 Tbsp baking powder
¼ tsp salt
½ tsp ground nutmeg
¼ tsp ground cinnamon
⅛ tsp ground cloves
1 tsp vanilla extract
½ cup dried tart cherries
½ cup golden raisins
grated zest of 1 lemon
1 seven-ounce package marzipan

Cream butter and sugar together until fluffy. Add eggs, one at a time, beating well after each addition. Sift together dry ingredients, and add to butter mixture, ⅓ at a time. Stir in vanilla, fruit, and zest. Pour half of batter into well-buttered 9-inch cake pan. Roll out marzipan into an 8-inch circle, and lay over batter in pan. Cover with remainder of batter, and bake at 300° for 1 hour 15 minutes, or until the cake springs back when lightly pressed.

CHAPTER 14
FATHER'S DAY
Date Varies

Father's Day began in the United States as a secular holiday, an equal-rights response to Mother's Day. As such, it dates back only to the late nineteenth century. Still, I am not the first to notice that the date falls close to the summer solstice, the day on which the Sun King reaches his zenith. Father's Day is the solstice brought to earth. On this day we honor both the father-principle of life and nature and the flesh-and-blood men who raised us.

In Finland, fathers receive the same honors on their day that mothers do in the U.S. Finnish children serve their fathers breakfast in bed, give them cards and gifts, and spend the day with them. Such rituals give the Fair Folk cause to laugh, as fatherhood counts little among them. The fathers among them tend not to be actively involved in raising their offspring. If they are widowers, they find a woman to raise their children, rather than nurture their children themselves.

In Nepal, Father's Day falls later in the summer, on the dark of the moon in late August or early September. People bring gifts and sweets to their fathers, and bow deeply before them in token of reverence. This human act mystifies the lesser species of Folk. The nobles among them, such as demigods and the ghosts of heroes, consider it perfectly appropriate.

Here in the U.S., some communities hold public barbecues on Father's Day. Other communities hold outdoor concerts, commonly jazz. Motorcycle clubs stage Father's Day runs. In these, all members are welcome to participate, without regard to gender or family status. As with all open parties, the Folk are likely to join in. Treat strangers kindly, as some of them may be more than human.

The most common tradition for the celebration of Father's Day is the same as for every other summer festival: the barbecue. The male head of household cooks meat over flames or glowing coals in his back yard, while the female head of household prepares salads in the kitchen. Our culture decrees that cooking outside is Man's Work, however rarely the same men cook indoors. Of course, not all men like to barbecue, and many others enjoy cooking, indoors or out, at any time of year. Let Dad choose for himself whether to participate in this annual rite. If he enjoys playing King of the Grill, so be it. Summer spirits enjoy a good barbecue. Leave an extra plate in an out-of-the-way place, for blessings and prosperity. If he would rather not cook, there are plenty of restaurants in the world that would be glad of the extra business.

Instead of focusing on the main meal, you could make Father's Day a Dad's Day Out with the whole family. Dad gets to choose the activity, whether he prefers a camping trip, a sporting event, or a trip to the local natural history museum. The important thing is that Dad gets to revel in his role as father of the family. Acknowledge his tie with the continuing chain of humanity, generation to generation, from the mythical past to the unknowable future. The world of Faerie is not exclusively feminine, as it is sometimes presented in picture books. The oak and the stag are as powerful in magic as the moon and the rose. Neglect them at your peril.

TRADITIONAL HOLIDAY FARE

GREEK CHICKEN

Serves 4

2 Tbsp olive oil

Juice of 1 lemon

2 cloves garlic, minced

½ tsp oregano

½ tsp salt

4 boneless, skinless chicken breasts

Combine first five ingredients. Pour over chicken and marinate overnight in refrigerator. If desired, grill over charcoal until meat is white throughout and juices run clear. Otherwise, bake at 400° for 30 minutes. Serve with rice.

CHAPTER 15
SUMMER SOLSTICE
On or Near June 21

The closer one gets to the Arctic Circle, the more vigorous the celebration of the summer solstice becomes. In the warm locales of the Mediterranean and the Caribbean, the solstice barely warrants a mention. In northern Europe, it rivals Christmas as the biggest event of the year.

Germans, Slavs, and Celts alike put together huge bonfires in recognition of the solstice. In Germany, Midsummer is seen as the time of the wedding of heaven and earth. Young people jump over fires to bring good luck and fertility. It is a time for love magic, love oracles, and fortune telling of all kinds. Love, magic, sex, and fertility are all concerns of the Folk. In the United States, it is a time for weddings. It is a time for cleaning out wells and springs, where the Good Folk gather. It is a time for public festivals.

I once spent a summer in a tiny village in Washington state where most of the population boasted Norwegian descent. At Midsummer, the whole town tried to stay up all night. We gathered at the big sauna by the creek, and told stories for as long as we could. It is hard to stay awake in a sauna late at night, and dangerous to go to sleep in one. Most of us declared victory after midnight, and went to bed. The Folk kept up the celebration without us, toasting in the sauna, plunging into the glacier-fed pool. The Folk enjoy all kinds of sensual pleasure, and have no need for sleep.

The Manx believe that mugwort, pulled up by its roots at midnight on Midsummer's Eve, will keep evil spirits away for an entire year.

The Irish keep their daughters inside on Midsummer Night, to prevent the Folk from claiming them as brides. The Sidhe have a high opinion of mortal women as wives and mothers, and eagerly marry them. These marriages end badly for the women involved, as the Folk have short attention spans where romance is involved. The most ardent of sweethearts, they are indifferent spouses. It is for the girls' protection that their parents keep them inside.

In Orkney, there are bonfires on Midsummer Eve. On the next morning, the people greet the sunrise with outstretched arms. As the seals in Iceland take human form on New Year's Eve, in Orkney they do the same at Midsummer. There is no distinction between common seals and the Selkies. All seals are enchanted beings, with immortal souls. While the Orcadians are ambivalent to mermaids and actively fear the Finmen, they love the Selkies. Love affairs and mixed marriages were common between Selkies and Orcadians in earlier times. To this day, webbed fingers and toes are seen as signs of Selkie ancestry.

Orcadians are divided about the origins of the Selkies, who are seals. Some say that when angels fell from heaven, the ones who fell onto land became the Fair Folk, while the ones who landed in the sea became Selkies. Some say that the Selkies were formerly men, who were transformed as punishment for their transgressions. Others say that the Selkies are the souls of human beings who were lost at sea.

In Finland, people clean house in preparation for Midsummer. As elsewhere, the Folk in the far north are sticklers for neatness. On Midsummer Eve, Finns have bonfires, as all far-northern peoples do. They eat dishes made with milk and eggs, in honor of farmers, and in gratitude to the Folk who bring abundance to the herds and flocks. Herring, potatoes, and schnapps are also traditional parts of the feast.

They hold the big party on the Saturday night closest to the solstice. Anyone who is able, leaves the city for the countryside. They visit relatives, play outdoor games, and attend music festivals. No one stays indoors who is able to be outdoors with the Folk. This is the best time of the year.

There are some Finnish rituals related to love and marriage that unmarried women perform at Midsummer. To a woman who gathers nine different kinds of wildflowers, puts them under her pillow, and goes to bed without speaking to anyone, the Folk will grant a dream of her future husband. If a woman runs naked through a field of rye, her true love will propose marriage.

One need do nothing special to attract the presence of the Folk at a Midsummer gathering. They will be there.

TRADITIONAL HOLIDAY FARE

JOCOQUE DULCE

Serves 4

This recipe was taught to me by a Mexican teenager who worked on the ranch where I was a cook. It was a favorite of his family and soon became a favorite throughout the ranch.

¼ cup brown sugar

1 cup sour cream

2 Tbsp dark rum, optional

½ tsp vanilla extract, optional

Mix thoroughly, and serve as a dip for all kinds of summer fruits.

CHAPTER 16
INDEPENDENCE DAY
July 4

There are no agriculture-based ethnic holidays in July, in the European tradition. This is the busy season for farmers in the temperate regions of the northern hemisphere. Taking a day off to party at this time would make as much sense to a farmer as closing up shop in December would make to a merchant. There will be plenty of time for parties after the harvest.

What we Americans have added to the worldwide bounty of fun is Independence Day. We have long since patched up the quarrel we had with England. We celebrate the Fourth of July without rancor, all in good fun.

While the lore of the Fourth is entirely concerned with human heroism, with nary a mention of participation by the Folk, Independence Day parties can be among the most magical. The key is to combine tradition with imagination.

The traditional parts of the Fourth are cookouts during the daylight hours and fireworks after dark. The imagination that can be added is infinite.

On one memorable Fourth, my high-school band traveled out of town, marching in several parades along the way. Our reward came that night, as we floated in a high-school swimming pool near the state capitol, while the municipal fireworks display went off directly overhead. The juxtaposition of fire and water charged the air with magic. The Folk were among us, whispering of love and mischief. The Folk frequently suggest love and mischief to teenagers.

Another particularly fine Fourth involved activities that were illegal, then as now. A hundred of us went to the beach in costume, accompanied by a case of home-brewed ale, several watermelons, and a pit-roasted pig. After the barbecue and the home-brew came the homemade fireworks, set off over the Pacific Ocean. Our reasoning behind the activity and the location was that we could set fire to neither sand nor water. Thousands of others, using similar powers of rationalization, made for a grand display of amateur pyrotechnics. More than one person, knowing the history of Chinese fireworks, said, "Well, the West Coast will be safe from invasion by demons this year." The Folk join in all open, outdoor parties, especially when the participants are masked. Under these circumstances, they are indistinguishable from plain people.

Alas, this has become part of the legendary past. I would not take so much as a bottle of beer to a public beach nowadays, let alone several boxes of skyrockets. Laws are enforced much more strictly these days.

At the time of the nation's Bicentennial, I was living in a tiny, remote mountain village, the same one where we tried to stay up all night at midsummer. The townsfolk painted every snowmobile in town red, white, and blue, and paraded them down the main, and only, street. The whole population, which may have been 500 (swelled by summer tourists), turned up for hamburgers grilled on the village green. It was a memorable day, even though unbroken forest put fireworks out of the question. The Folk in attendance were Nordic, as were most of the human beings. They enjoyed meat grilled outdoors—a sign, by their customs, of royal hospitality.

More recently, I had a friend who lived on a street that led directly to the hill from which the municipal fireworks were fired. Every year, he invited all his friends and relatives for an all-day barbecue. As the time for fireworks approached, we set up our chairs on his front lawn, to watch the show. The official display only lasted ten or fifteen minutes. The sport of the evening was counting the brushfires that resulted, watching the lights of the fire trucks snaking up the narrow road, and speculating whether the trucks would reach the fires before the fires reached the expensive houses on the side of the hill.

My friend no longer lives there, but I have checked with the local newspaper in that town. They still set the hill on fire every year. Instead of the night of the iguana, they have the night of the salamander, the elemental spirit of fire.

INDEPENDENCE DAY

Each year, the firemen narrowly turn back the salamanders. The friendly Folk had been among us, not knowing which side to take. The hamburgers enticed them to our side.

Wherever people are laughing, eating, wallowing in tradition or tweaking tradition on the nose, the friendly Folk join us, laughing by our sides.

CHAPTER 17
COLD CHRISTMAS
CAMPERS' CHRISTMAS
July 25

COLD CHRISTMAS

In Australia, December 25 falls during hot weather. They manage a roast and a plum pudding, but the weather is too hot to properly enjoy an old-fashioned British Christmas. For this reason, many Aussies put together a proper Christmas party in July, when it is cold enough to eat large quantities of the rich foods Christmas demands.

The frequent contact between Celts and Vikings in the Middle Ages populated the British Isles with Nordic sprites, including Elves and *Nisses*. They traveled with the Britons and Celts, when these people settled Australia. They regret the loss of a proper Christmas, with a roast goose and many rich desserts. A feast, once the weather turns cold, helps make up the loss.

CAMPERS' CHRISTMAS

Canada has no lack of snow and ice in December. In some parts of Canada, people celebrate Campers' Christmas in July, for the opposite reason Aussies celebrate Cold Christmas. Campers' Christmas gives Canadians an excuse to have big picnic dinners, and throw big parties outdoors.

Any of the menus and party plans listed under Christmas would be appropriate for a Christmas in July party. Feel free to throw one, if you feel festivity-deprived in the summer. For a Campers' Christmas, arrange for a group campsite at any park or national forest that allows camping. Tell as many of your friends as the site will hold that you have reserved the site for the night, and you are planning a party. This would be a good occasion for a potluck, as catering an event out of a camper or tent would be beyond the abilities of most people. All outdoor parties attract the Folk. Far from the city, you may meet a wilder sort than you would in your own garden. Do not wander alone too far in the dark.

Be sure to find out whether open campfires will be allowed. Rules change frequently, according to the fire danger in any given season. Running for your life sucks the festivity out of any occasion.

Be sure to celebrate in proper style. Decorate your campsite. Dress up as Santa Claus. Have a great time. At the edge of the circle of light thrown by your campfire, you will see woodland creatures-squirrels, owls, perhaps. These are the Folk, in disguise. Honor them with your love.

Remember that joy expands outwards, affecting every being within range for the better. The Folk will share your joy and return it, multiplied.

TRADITIONAL HOLIDAY FARE

FRESNO GELATIN

Serves 8

This is the sort of silly, old-fashioned dish that always appeared at potluck suppers forty years ago. It tastes as good now as it ever did, and has acquired a retro appeal.

1 20-ounce can crushed pineapple, drained, juice reserved

1 large package lime-flavored gelatin dessert mix, to make 8
    servings

Juice reserved from pineapple, plus enough water to total 3
    cups liquid

1 cup heavy whipping cream, whipped

1 cup shredded coconut

Dissolve gelatin dessert mix into 2 cups boiling pineapple liquid, as directed on box. Add the additional 1 cup of liquid, cold, and place in refrigerator until slightly thickened. When slightly thickened, fold in pineapple, whipped cream, and coconut. Chill until firm.

CHAPTER 18
LAMMAS

August 1

Lammas is one of the holidays that have been nearly forgotten in the U.S. It is a harvest festival. We have folded all of the minor harvest festivals into the grand glutton's feast of Thanksgiving. Why eat yourself sick on one day, when you can eat yourself happy at several smaller feasts throughout the harvest season?

Lammas is the festival of loaves, honoring the first grain harvest of autumn. While it falls during the hottest part of the summer, it is an autumn festival, just as Imbolc, in early February, is a spring festival. Old Europe counted the seasons differently than we do. The summer solstice is called, on our calendars, "The first day of summer," but in Europe, the same day is celebrated as Midsummer Day. Similarly, the winter solstice is the first day of winter here, Midwinter Day there.

Lammas is also Lughnasa, the festival of the ancient Celtic god of light. The sun is still high at Lammas, the days long and hot. The Sun King still reigns. While few now remember the rites of Lugh, he should still be held in honor as a king among the Folk.

Orcadians advise people to put four-leafed clovers in their shoes on this day, to protect them from the wiles of con artists and swindlers. They do not specify the nature of these malefactors, but four-leafed clovers are well-known protection against being taken in by fairy glamour.

Bake bread in fancy shapes. Make one more loaf than you will need, and leave it outside for the use of the Folk. Appropriate designs are crowns, sheaves of grain, or women or men dressed in folk costumes. If shaping a loaf free-form is beyond your level of culinary comfort, use a mold. Appropriately shaped molds are available in gourmet shops, or by mail.

A bonfire is a suitable activity for Lammas, if you have a place and a permit. If you have a bonfire, save a branch from the fire. If you keep the branch in the house, the Folk will protect the house from lightning for the rest of the year.

A harvest party is a good way to celebrate Lammas. Get up an expedition of friends and family to a you-pick farm. Cook up part of the harvest afterward, to share among yourselves. Craft festivals are also traditional, and more common than you might guess. Your local newspaper will probably reveal one within easy driving distance, on or near August 1. Pick up something for the Folk to enjoy, such as a birdhouse, a feeder, or an ornament for the garden.

This is how we connect with the seasons, with the earth, with the spiritual nature of our surroundings.

This is how we connect with the Folk.

TRADITIONAL HOLIDAY FARE

LAMMAS BREAD

Makes 1 large or 2 regular loaves

2 cups whole wheat flour

2 cups bread flour, plus more if needed

¼ cup toasted sesame seeds

2 Tbsp active dry yeast

2 ½ tsp salt

2 cups milk, scalded

3 Tbsp smooth peanut butter

3 Tbsp honey

Mix dry ingredients in large bowl. Add peanut butter and honey to hot milk and stir to combine. Cool milk mixture to very warm, approximately 115°.

Stir milk mixture into flour mixture. Knead for 15 minutes, adding enough additional flour to make a smooth, elastic dough. Oil the surface of the dough, cover with plastic wrap or a damp tea towel, and let rise in a warm place until double in bulk. Punch it down, shape it into two rectangular loaves or one large wreath, and let rise again until doubled. Bake in a pre-heated 375° oven until golden brown, and it sounds hollow when you tap it on the bottom.

CHAPTER 19
LABOR DAY
Date Varies

On the first Monday in September, we honor the working class by giving them the day off from work. That was the intention, at least. Now, there are enough classifications of people who must work, without regard for holidays, that only a minority of people get to spend the day at leisure.

Ironically, leisure is the essence of Labor Day. While our calendars proclaim the end of summer still three weeks away, our culture celebrates Labor Day as the last true day of summer. It is not the agricultural summer that ends on Labor Day, but the summer of our youth, when school was out and our days were our own. Labor Day is a time for picnics, for campouts, for baseball games, for one last fling in the open air before we have to get back to our desks.

What a shame that the campgrounds are full. Pack a basket, or grill something in your own back yard. I am going to let you in on a secret: you do not have to join, lemming-like, in the mob that fills the national parks. Enjoy Labor Day at home. Make friends with the Folk who live in your yard. If you are in one of those jobs that must be filled at all times, volunteer to work on Labor Day, in exchange for another day off. Make your own three-day weekend, whenever you please. Then you may go camping, without having to face traffic jams in the park. You will have the Fair Folk to yourself. They dislike being crowded, and will reveal themselves to you in the quiet of autumn.

TRADITIONAL HOLIDAY FARE

POTATO SALAD
FOR A CROWD

Serves 40

This recipe will require the use of your biggest kettle to cook the potatoes, and a big hotel pan to mix the salad. Disposable aluminum hotel pans are available in wholesale grocery stores, if you do not want to invest in a steel one.

The personality of this salad reflects the mustard you use. Pick one that will be popular with the crowd.

10 pounds russet potatoes, whole and unpeeled

1 dozen eggs

1 bunch celery

2 bunches green onions

1 large red onion

1 quart jar dill pickles

2 large cucumbers

1 quart mayonnaise

1 quart unflavored yogurt

1 12-ounce jar mustard

2 Tbsp salt

1 Tbsp ground black pepper

1 Tbsp granulated garlic

Boil the potatoes in their skins until tender when pierced, about half an hour after they come to a boil. Drain. When cool enough to handle, peel and dice them. Hard cook the eggs, by covering them with cool water, bringing them to a boil, and simmering them for 10 minutes. Peel and dice the eggs, and add them to the potatoes. Finely dice the remaining vegetables, and mix with the potatoes and eggs. In a separate bowl, mix the remaining ingredients. Carefully fold the dressing into the potato mixture. Serve chilled or at room temperature.

CHAPTER 20
HARVEST HOME
Approximately September 21

The autumnal equinox falls on or near September 21, but the date of Harvest Home varies according to locale. The proper time for a harvest festival is when the crops have just been harvested, and are therefore most abundant.

Some time between late September and early October, Germans celebrate their harvest festival, *Erntefest*. All of these festivals are thrown in honor of the Folk, the nature spirits who bring fertility. Some towns set the date according to the day of the week, others by the phase of the moon. However they set the date, they will throw dances, parades, sporting events, feasts, and pageants. Oxen, decorated with flowers and ribbons, will pull a decorated wagon full of grain. A figure woven of grain, and dressed as a woman, will ride on top of this wagon. This is the Corn Mother, common to both Germanic and Celtic tradition, who embodies the spirit of the crop. In some towns, people throw buckets of water at the wagon to ensure adequate rainfall for the next year's crop. In others, a real girl represents the spirit of the crop, and is similarly drenched.

The Corn Mother is never neglected or thrown away after the celebration. The love and honor the people have for the Folk is shown to the Corn Mother. In some areas, she is returned to the fields to ensure a good crop next year. In some, she is fed to the livestock, to make them fertile. Her grain may be mixed with the seed corn, for luck. She may be given intact to the slowest worker on the farm, to shame him into working faster. In some areas, she is thrown into the river, to bring rain. No disrespect is intended by this, but acknowledgment that water brings life. She may be hung from the rafters, to protect against evil influences. She may be burned, and the ashes from her funeral pyre scattered over the fields, that she may return in the form of next year's crop.

The ancient Norse made bread in the shape of the gods, and gave it to the Elves. Modern Swedes make this bread in the shape of a girl, and share it among the family.

Everywhere, the first fruits of the harvest are offered to someone important. This may be the king, the gods, the spirits of the crops, the spirits of the ancestors. Except for a mortal king, these are all representatives of the Folk. The Folk express thanks for the gift by continuing to bring good weather and rich harvests.

In France and Germany, people bring the Harvest May into the house. This is a tree or large branch that protects the home against lightning, fire, and all harm. Like the Christmas tree, the Harvest May is a home for the Folk, a place where they may be warm and secure for the winter. When they move into a home, they protect it as their own. This is a good use for a potted citrus tree that will not survive winter in the cold. Put it in a sunny window as a blessing on the home. Depending on the variety, it may give you fresh fruit for Christmas, which is a blessing in itself. Nagami kumquat is especially good as a potted tree, to provide a fairy habitat indoors. It is beautiful, fragrant, and small, and it bears tasty fruit in winter. It looks like an elfin orange tree.

The German *Oktoberfest* is a special example of a harvest feast. It was originally celebrated as a royal wedding in 1810, but everyone had such a good time that they decided to do it every year. For two weeks, beginning at the autumnal equinox, Germans devote themselves to eating, drinking, and dancing to traditional music. In addition, there are horse races and agricultural fairs, which are favorite pastimes of the Folk.

The full moon nearest the autumnal equinox, which we call the Harvest Moon, is especially prized in Japan. The Japanese hold moon-viewing parties at this time, to appreciate the special beauty of the Harvest Moon, and to give thanks for the harvest. Think how lovely it would be to throw a formal picnic at night, under the full moon. Such a picnic would be a festive occasion for many-or a romantic one, for two. The *Kami*, the spirit-people of

Japan, will be among you. Do not worry about cooking. For such an important holiday, any Asian market will stock appropriate delicacies.

The Kami are fanatical about cleanliness. Be sure your site is clean before you summon them. To summon the Kami, wash your hands and brush your teeth. Place food on an altar or stone. Clap your hands twice, bow twice, and clap your hands again. You may then ask a favor of them, if you like. The Kami like parades, music, and dolls. Mirrors and reflecting pools also attract them. While some can be treacherous, most Kami are entirely benevolent.

Except for the Kami you have summoned, do not let the Folk catch you looking for them. The Folk dance in the moonlight, and do not want to be disturbed. For the Folk as well as for ourselves, this may be the last holiday of the year on which it is warm enough to dance outdoors.

Orkney has some distinctive traditions regarding the last sheaf of wheat to be harvested. On some islands, the last worker to come in from the fields is spanked with it. Its grain is then made into bread, which is given to the man who was spanked. He gets a running head start, after which his coworkers give chase, trying to get the bread away from him.

On other islands in Orkney, the last man in from the fields has to climb the tallest haystack in the barn, while his coworkers try to catch him. If he makes it to the top of the haystack, the boss gives him a loaf of bread and a bottle of beer. If his coworkers catch him first, they pull down his pants and cover his bottom with molasses.

The farm workers of Orkney have great incentive to work quickly, to avoid being the last man finished. It is a great responsibility to be the last man. The spirit of the crop resides in the last sheaf to be harvested, and then transfers to the last man working. The playful humiliation of a spanking or an anointing with molasses represents a sacrifice of the spirit of the crop to the greater spirit of Nature, in expectation of continued prosperity. All of this is done in honor of the Folk.

The stormy weather Orkney suffers in September is explained as evidence of battles fought between the Selkies and the Folk of the land. If drought threatens, it would be a good idea at this time to stage a mock battle between the Sea-people and the Land-people, represented by yourselves, to encourage rain. The land team should use foam-rubber weapons, to avoid real injuries resulting from your mock battle. The Selkie team should throw water around, using hoses, buckets, and pump-activated water guns, to give the Folk the idea of rain.

It is appropriate, at harvest time, to share from your abundance. In Ireland, people who are doing well give gifts of goose and mutton to the poor. In the United States, we begin our canned food drives, the food to be distributed at Thanksgiving and Christmas. Most homeless shelters and similar charities are overwhelmed with donations during the holidays, but understocked the rest of the year. Give now, and beat the Christmas rush. Make a commitment to give to charity throughout the year. The Folk love generosity, and reward it lavishly.

TRADITIONAL HOLIDAY FARE

HUNTERS' STEW

Serves 8

1 quart good-quality sauerkraut
1 onion, thinly sliced
1 pound smoked sausage, cut into 2-inch lengths
1 pound cooked turkey, diced
1 pound cooked pork, diced

Place sauerkraut in bottom of large, nonreactive saucepan. Layer onions over it, then meats. Cover and steam over low heat for 45 minutes. Serve over mashed potatoes.

SWEET AND SOUR RED CABBAGE

Serves 6

This is just the thing to go with schnitzel, or sausage and potatoes.

¼ cup butter
1 large onion, diced
1 head red cabbage, shredded
2 apples, sliced
½ tsp salt
¼ cup vinegar
¼ cup brown sugar

In nonreactive pan, sauté onions in butter until transparent. Add remaining ingredients, cover, and simmer until as done as you want them: from at least 40 minutes to as long as 3 hours!

CHAPTER 21
HALLOWEEN
October 31

Halloween, or All Hallows' Eve, is generally regarded as secular, even though it is named in honor of All Saints' Day, November 1. Wherever people celebrate Halloween, they are participating in a feast celebrating the Celtic New Year. While most American holiday customs are of German origin, Halloween is Irish. Goblins and ghosts and lanterns carved out of vegetables came over early, and were reinforced with the waves of migration during the Hunger.

The old Celtic name for Halloween is Samhain, pronounced "sowen," or "sawven." It means "Summer's End," and marks the time for threshing grain and preparing food for winter storage. The cattle were brought into the barns for the winter, as killing frosts could occur at any time from then on.

On Halloween, the spirits of dead relatives visit their families, looking for warmth and cheer. As some cultures maintain that the dead prefer round food, popcorn balls and caramel apples are appropriate foods to have available for them. The Fair Folk change their lodgings at this time, coming and going as they please. If you desire to share your home with the Folk, this is the time to invite them. Have food and beverages available to them-water, milk, perhaps beer or whiskey, along with sweets and buttered bread. Human beings who have been kidnapped by the Folk can be rescued on Halloween. Look for them in your dreams. They will instruct you in how to rescue them. The technique is different in every case.

Being at the turn of the Celtic year, Halloween belongs to neither the old year nor the new. What people do on Halloween does not count; it is a time for breaking taboos. Children may run around unsupervised, and eat all the candy they can hold. If they adorn a neighbor's tree with toilet paper, or put toothpaste on a doorknob, they will receive no worse punishment than a scolding. Adults can dress as ghosts, vampires, or animals, even at work.

While our American custom of trick-or-treating only goes back as far as the 1930s, its Irish roots go back hundreds of years. Irish people used to beg door to door for party supplies, offering a prayer in exchange for donations of food, beverages, or money. They expected the Folk to attend their parties. The Folk were their daily companions, never far away or absent for long.

No fire was permitted to travel from the old year into the new. All fires were extinguished, and a new fire lit by striking flints. This new fire was then used to light all the necessary fires for the coming year; it was kept burning continually. I once had a roommate who used the pilot light on his stove for this purpose. Few now remember or practice this tradition. As we replace our old appliances with more efficient, pilotless designs, it is likely to die out entirely.

Halloween had itself nearly died out in the British Isles, until it was reintroduced by Americans. The British now indulge in costumes and merrymaking, but without the trick-or-treating and vandalism.

The Fair Folk and the spirits of the dead dance together in graveyards on Halloween. People must exercise extreme caution around graveyards on Halloween, as the Folk will attempt to kidnap human musicians to play for their dances. To any mortal musician who plays for them, the Folk will teach their melodies. Tales tell of many traditional Irish airs that originated in Faerie. If a mortal musician wishes to play for a fairy dance, he should remember that an overnight visit to the kingdom of Faerie will equal an absence of a year from the mortal realm.

In Germany, farm animals talk on this night, as they are associated with the Folk. It is considered rude for people to listen. Children engage in some minor mischief, in some districts.

In ancient times, Romans adopted the Celtic celebration of Samhain, and combined it with their festival of Pomona, goddess of the harvest. Apples were sacred to Pomona. This may be the origin of such Halloween practices as bobbing for apples. All fruit that remains on the trees after Halloween belongs to the Folk. To an unmarried woman who holds an apple in one hand and a mirror in the other, the Folk will give a vision of her future husband.

Alas, perceived danger is killing off Halloween even in its more recent forms. Hordes of unsupervised children no longer rule the early evening, having fallen victim to urban legends about razor blades in apples and needles in candy bars. Trick-or-treating is becoming more common in malls than in neighborhoods. Trick-or-treating from store to store is not much fun, and the Folk do not frequent commercial centers. Trick-or-treating is being replaced with private parties. Parties are a good thing, as long as children still get a chance to play at being pirates and witches and princesses, and as long as they get to eat more sugar than is strictly healthy. Telling fortunes and ghost stories, traditional activities at Halloween parties, are effective means of gaining the attention and participation of the Folk.

TRADITIONAL HOLIDAY FARE

HOT APPLE CIDER

Serves 20

Use dealcoholized wine if any of your guests should not have alcohol. This drink is good for every party from Halloween through Yule.

1 gallon apple juice
1 bottle dry white wine
1 orange
1 Tbsp whole cloves
2 cinnamon sticks

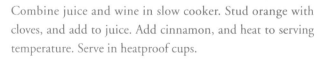

Combine juice and wine in slow cooker. Stud orange with cloves, and add to juice. Add cinnamon, and heat to serving temperature. Serve in heatproof cups.

If you have leftovers, strain out spices before storing cider in refrigerator, so the flavors do not become too strong.

CHAPTER 22
DAYS OF THE DEAD
November 1 and 2

Mexico has a unique way of celebrating All Souls' Day. It combines the Catholic feast day with ancient indigenous beliefs to create a multigenerational family reunion, at which the guests are not limited to the living. Indeed, the most welcome guests are friendly ghosts and the Folk, who are indistinguishable.

Just as white butterflies embody the souls of the dead in Ireland, monarch butterflies do so in Mexico. Monarch butterflies migrate through much of North America, leaving the northern areas in the summer to reach Mexico in the fall. Mexicans welcome the bright orange monarchs, their departed relatives, with displays of bright orange marigolds at the beginning of November.

On November 1, they welcome the souls of departed children, with candy skulls and feasts of the child's favorite foods, as at a birthday party. On November 2, departed adults are honored, with graveside picnics. The dead are given food and tequila. None of this is in the character of mourning; it is a party, a festive opportunity to visit with relatives who have been out of touch. Do not think of them as objects of fear, but as friends on the other side of the veil, inhabitants of Faerie.

TRADITIONAL HOLIDAY FARE

PAN DE LOS MUERTOS: BREAD OF THE DEAD

Makes 1 large or 3 small loaves

While many Mexican panes dulces (sweet breads) are heavy and dull, this is light and fragrant. Make only the best for the dear departed.

1 cup milk

½ cup butter

1 ½ cups all-purpose flour

2 Tbsp active dry yeast

1 tsp salt

1 Tbsp anise seed

½ cup granulated sugar

4 eggs

4 additional cups all-purpose flour, approximately

Scald milk, add butter, and set aside.

In a large mixing bowl, mix 1 ½ cups of flour with yeast, salt, anise seed, and sugar.

In a small mixing bowl, beat eggs. Slowly add milk mixture, beating constantly. Your object is to warm the eggs and cool the milk, so the yeast will be happy.

Beat the egg mixture into the flour mixture. Add the additional flour, 1 cup at a time, beating well after each addition. Once a soft dough forms, knead for 10 minutes.

Oil surface of dough, cover with plastic wrap or a damp tea towel, and allow to rise in a warm place until doubled in bulk. Punch down, and shape into a ball. If you wish, pinch off a couple of small pieces of dough, shape them into bones, and lay them over the top of the round loaf. Cover, and allow to rise until again doubled in bulk. Bake in a pre-heated 350° oven for 40 minutes, until beautifully golden, and it sounds hollow when you tap it on the bottom. If you prefer to shape it into 3 smaller loaves, bake them at 400°, and check them after 20 minutes.

CHAPTER 23
ST. MARTIN'S DAY
November 11

Although it is still more than a month until Christmas, in Germany, St. Martin's Day marks the beginning of preparations for Carnival. They celebrate it as a holiday in its own right. Children sing in the streets, and adults give them sweets. Later, there are bonfires, and a feast of roast goose.

St. Martin's Day is a good excuse to throw a big feed and invite friends who will be unable to join you for Thanksgiving, due to family commitments. Similarly, if you will be a guest at someone else's table for Thanksgiving, St. Martin's Day is your chance to roast a really big bird. The Folk are always glad of a festive occasion and a free meal.

The weather is getting colder. If you have not already brought in your tender plants for the winter, bring them in now, as a winter resort for the Folk.

TRADITIONAL HOLIDAY FARE

ROAST GOOSE

Serves 6

½ cup granulated sugar
½ cup salt
1 cup lemon juice or vinegar
1 quart water
1 twelve-pound goose
water to cover goose

In a nonreactive pan large enough to hold the goose, mix sugar, salt, lemon juice or vinegar, and the first quantity of water. Stir until dissolved. Put the goose in the brine, and add enough water to cover the goose. Refrigerate overnight.

Roast goose on a rack in a roasting pan, uncovered, for 1 hour at 400º. Turn heat down to 325º, and roast for another 1½ hours, until leg wobbles in joint when tested. Let it rest at room temperature for 10–20 minutes before carving.

CHAPTER 24
THANKSGIVING
Date Varies

Elementary schools throughout the land spread the myth that the First Thanksgiving was celebrated by Pilgrims and Native Americans together in 1621. In fact, Thanksgiving feasts go back much farther than that. Native Americans did not wait for the English to instruct them in the ways of gratitude. The Iroquois, as one example, had a Thanksgiving feast every month during the growing season. They had feasts and rituals for each successive harvest, from strawberries in June to ripe corn in October, followed by a grand feast in thanks for all the harvests in November.

As is true everywhere, the Folk native to the Americas are of an ambivalent nature. In order to be sure of friendly treatment, greet them politely, treat them kindly, and give them something good to eat. They favor foods native to North America, such as baked salmon and blueberry pie.

When camping, in order not to inadvertently snub any Folk within earshot, say, "Goodnight" to everyone and everything that might be listening. One Native American girl, the story goes, said, "Goodnight to all the lovely things." A troll-like creature whose name was Ugly Thing overheard, and took offense. It took several days for the girl to convince Ugly Thing that she had not meant to hurt his feelings.

According to the stories, Native Americans discovered something Europeans have never known: how to have a happy, lasting marriage with one of the Folk. The secret is for the human partner to leave earth and go to live in Faerie. No native of Faerie has yet adjusted to living full-time on earth. People who go to the Faerie eventually adapt, and take on fairy natures themselves, if they do not succumb to homesickness. A woman who married a merman turned into a kindly sea serpent. A man who married a Star Maiden had human form while in Faerie, but took the form of a white falcon to visit his human relatives.

In the early days of English settlement in North America, Thanksgiving was the most popular date for weddings. Farming people were much too busy from spring until harvest to take the time for such things as wedding feasts and honeymoons. By Thanksgiving, the harvest was over, the family had gathered, and there would be plenty of leisure time for the bride and groom to become acquainted as wife and husband.

Different towns celebrated Thanksgiving by local proclamation, on different days, as they do in Germany to this day. Only at the time of the Civil War did Thanksgiving become a national holiday, by presidential proclamation.

The main dishes of early Thanksgiving dinners sound good: fish, turkey, goose, venison. The actual recipes used were grim. One early recipe for turkey called for stuffing it with a mixture of oatmeal and onions. Gravy was a mixture of turkey drippings and vinegar. I will spare you the recipes for boiled fish, boiled pumpkin, boiled cole slaw (honest!), wheat pudding, and prune pie. I am sorry lobster got dropped from the menu, though. Once the settlers could provide enough meat from farm animals to feed everyone present, they decided to abstain from buggy things with lots of legs, picked off the shore. Funny how one era's subsistence rations become another era's luxuries. Their religion was as grim as their recipes. Rather than deny the existence of the Folk, they identified them as demons. People who sought the company of the Folk were ostracized, or killed.

Today, turkey is the almost invariant centerpiece of the Thanksgiving feast in the United States. Even strict vegetarians can have a turkey dinner, as markets catering to vegetarians mold tofu into the shape of turkeys at this time of year. The other dishes on the table reflect the tastes and ethnicities of the people present. An American family of Italian descent might serve antipasto, pasta, artichokes, and mushrooms with their turkey. In deference to my mother's Caribbean tastes, my family always had baked yams, which were never candied, and a molded gelatin salad, in addition to all the usual American

Thanksgiving dishes. Serve the foods of your heritage. This will signal the Folk native to your ancestral home that they are welcome.

As an addition or alternative to the usual American Thanksgiving, there is Diwali, the Hindu Thanksgiving. The honor is given to Lakshmi, the beautiful goddess of luck and prosperity. Lakshmi is made of rose petals. Like the Folk, she embodies beauty and wishes.

Diwali falls in late October or early November. The celebrants clean house thoroughly. The oldest woman sweeps the floor, to sweep away the bad luck. People decorate their homes with flowers, make sweets, and visit with their friends and relatives. To encourage prosperity, they decorate their houses with symbols of prosperity, such as toy cars and play money. They exchange cards and gifts. In the evening, they have fireworks displays. Girls and women float oil lamps on the river. It is a sign of good luck for the lamps to reach the other side. Men gamble, to display their faith in the goddess of luck.

When performing rites near water, especially lily ponds, be mindful of the *apsaras*. These celestial water-nymphs are native to India, but have also been present from Tibet to China and Ceylon for many hundreds of years. They have the beauty of divinity, as can be seen from their many painted and sculpted images in the East. They are givers of luck, pleasure, and blessing, when treated well. When treated badly, they bring insanity and death by drowning. Treat them with respect and consideration. To summon apsaras, float flowers on water, and play Indian music. Serve vegetarian foods rich in dairy products.

How lovely it would be, to decorate with flowers and candles, to play cards with your friends after a fine vegetarian meal. The Folk would find such an evening irresistible. What honors one being of beauty and peace, honors all.

TRADITIONAL HOLIDAY FARE

ROAST TURKEY

Allow one pound per serving

Many people of my generation and younger remember how hard our mothers and grandmothers worked at Thanksgiving. In consequence, many of us are afraid to tackle a turkey. We believe that there is some mystic secret involved, and an inordinate amount of hard work.

When I was a ranch cook, I made three turkeys per week for four years. That is over 600 turkeys. Consider another hundred or so that I have cooked for family and friends, and you would have to admit that I know turkey.

Here is the mystic secret: There is nothing easier than cooking a turkey. What made Thanksgiving dinner such an ordeal for our foremothers was the plethora of side dishes. Mashed potatoes, sweet potatoes, bread dressing, three hot vegetables, three salads, gravy, relishes, and at least two desserts were the causes of Grandmama's frazzled nerves. Simplify the menu. Accompany the turkey with one salad, one starchy side dish, and one vegetable, and you can feed the masses with no more anxiety than you expend on any Sunday supper. With fewer side dishes, you and your guests will have more room for those two or more desserts.

1 turkey, fresh or thoroughly defrosted
Granulated garlic
Ground black pepper

Rinse the turkey inside and out with cold running water. Sprinkle all surfaces with garlic and pepper. Place, breast side down, in covered enamelware roaster. Cover and cook at 325° for 15 minutes per pound. The bird is done when the skin is brown, and the leg joints move easily.

Transfer the turkey onto a serving platter and allow to rest at room temperature while you make the gravy.

GRAVY

Turkey drippings
Turkey or chicken stock
1 cup flour
1 cup water

Skim fat from surface of turkey drippings. Pour drippings into saucepan, and add enough stock to make as much gravy as you need. The higher the proportion of drippings to stock, the better the gravy will taste. A 20-pound bird will provide enough drippings to make two quarts of delicious gravy. Bring dripping/stock mixture to a boil. Whisk flour and water together in a small bowl until smooth. Whisk this mixture, which fancy chefs call a "slurry," and rough-and-ready cooks call a "whitewash," slowly into the boiling stock mixture, until it is as thick as you want it. Let it simmer 3 minutes more, to get rid of the raw taste of the flour.

Since you prepared the rest of the dinner while the turkey was in the oven, dinner is now ready to serve.

KHIR INDIAN RICE PUDDING

Serves 6

1 ½ cups cooked basmati rice
1 twelve-ounce can evaporated milk
1 fourteen-ounce can sweetened condensed milk
1 pinch saffron
½ tsp ground cardamom
½ cup finely chopped almonds
½ cup finely chopped cashews

Mix all ingredients in heavy saucepan. Bring to a boil, over low heat, stirring constantly. Turn heat to very low, and simmer 10 minutes. Serve warm or cool.

Lakshmi's Pistachio Ice Cream

Makes 1 ½ quarts

This ice cream is insanely delicious. It is made with canned milk products, due to the history and climate of India. In the tropics, without access to refrigeration, fresh milk exists more in theory than in fact. What is not canned rapidly converts to yogurt.

This recipe freezes rock-hard, so, if you do not eat it up as soft serve, freeze it in a shallow container. To serve, run a knife under hot water, and cut the ice cream into serving portions.

Do not add eggs to this recipe, in order to improve the texture. Eggs are forbidden by Hindu dietary principles.

1 pinch saffron
1 tsp water
1 12-ounce can evaporated milk
1 pint heavy cream
1 14-ounce can sweetened condensed milk
¾ cup natural shelled pistachios
½ tsp ground cardamom

Soak saffron in water for 10 minutes. Put all ingredients together in blender, and whir until pistachios are well ground. Freeze in ice cream freezer according to manufacturer's directions. Serve immediately, or turn into a shallow container to freeze solid. May be frozen in ice pop molds, if desired.

CHAPTER 25
WINTER SOLSTICE
Approximately December 21
CHRISTMAS
December 25
YULE
Either Date

I combine the holidays of Christmas and the winter solstice, because they should be one. The date of Christmas was set at the winter solstice 1,600 years ago, in order to combine Pagan and Christian festivities. Calendrical variations since then have caused December 25 to move away from the solstice.

In any case, the term "Yule" can be applied to either date. Whether it is Christmas or Yule that we celebrate, the midwinter holiday is the greatest cultural festival in the United States or Europe. The celebrations go on for over a month, from the day after Thanksgiving until the children return to school after New Year's Day. Many businesses close for the week between Christmas and New Year's Day, and most schools close for at least two weeks.

In practice, the preparations for Yule can go on for the entire year. Many thrifty souls take pride in stocking up on cards, wrapping paper, and gifts during the clearance sales that follow Christmas. We keep our eyes open for just the right gifts for our friends throughout the year, for giving in December. Handmade gifts must be started by August, in order to allow time for completion.

There is a lot going on. The Folk are intimately involved in every phase of preparation and celebration. This is the liveliest part of their year, as it is of ours.

YULE—THE ANCIENT PAST

ROME

Saturnalia was celebrated in ancient Rome from approximately December 17 until December 24. Roman slaves had the time off, with their masters waiting on them. The Romans honored *Sol Invictus*, the Unconquered Sun, at this time. This was indeed a show of faith, as the sun could appear close to defeat at the time of the winter solstice. To show your faith that long, sunny days will resume, light candles. If you have a fireplace, light a fire. While not part of our usual American decorations, sun faces can be incorporated into the Yule decorations, to good effect.

One year I took the theme of warmth and sunshine as far as it would go, for my Yule party. With my husband's assistance, I designed an invitation showing Santa's sleigh flying over a tropical island. I encouraged my guests to wear Hawaiian shirts, and served foods indigenous to Jamaica, Cuba, and Puerto Rico. I bought fabric in wild tropical prints, and made tablecloths from it. The biggest hit of the evening was the *coquito*, the coconut eggnog. My front porch was full of tropical plants, sheltering from winter frosts. Toy tree frogs adorned the bananas and gingers. Santa peeked out from behind a fern. Decorative elves were present, which I had not placed. Flamingos appeared on my lawn. Some of the mischief and merriment can be credited to my human friends, but some is yet unexplained.

Most of the customs of Saturnalia, such as public nudity, heavy drinking, dancing in the streets, and reversal of social roles, have been moved to Carnival. The Church considered these carryings-on inappropriate, once they set the birthday of Jesus at the winter solstice. You can't act that way with a newborn in the house.

THE BRITISH ISLES

Even before Christianization, the Celts in the British Isles decorated their homes with holly, mistletoe, and other evergreens at the winter solstice. They also burned bonfires and Yule logs, to strengthen and encourage the sun, weak at this time of year. The custom of the Yule log, the only ritual bonfire to be burned indoors, is waning due to the decrease in the size of domestic fireplaces. One can burn a tree trunk in a castle fireplace the size of a modern living room, but not in a brick-lined box the size of a microwave oven. The

Yule log makes its symbolic appearance in the form of a cake. The Folk do not mind the substitution, as long as there is plenty of greenery and plenty to eat.

In the Middle Ages, Christmas was a huge celebration. It featured not only overeating, singing, dancing, sporting events, and costume balls, but also wassailing, a festive begging of food and drink. The feasts included roast peacock as well as roast beef and salmon pies. When the Puritans took over the government of England in the 1640s, they banned Christmas by act of Parliament. The Puritans considered the friendly association of people and the Folk to be demonic. The populace reacted by rioting. Charles II reinstated Christmas, but it did not regain its previous level of popularity until the nineteenth century. That was when Queen Victoria's Prince Albert brought German holiday customs with him to England. To this day, Christmas celebrations in England and America are more continental in character than English.

While wassailing was a form of begging, apple wassailing was and is a means of giving back to the community of Fair Folk. The Folk habitually reward generosity with generosity, and the Folk control the fertility of the crops. People would sing songs to an apple tree, a favorite of the Folk, and pour cider over it. They did this to encourage the tree to fruit well the following year.

The British Father Christmas is not related to Saint Nicholas, Bishop of Myra, but descends directly from Pagan folk tradition. Prior to the nineteenth century, Father Christmas was more concerned with drinking and entertaining women than with bringing presents to children.

In Britain, there is a whole series of customs surrounding mincemeat pies. The English make a wish on the first mince pie of the season. They make it a practice to eat a mince pie on each of the Twelve Days of Christmas, from Christmas to Epiphany, January 6. They bring mince pies to everyone they visit during this period, and every visitor is also given a mince pie. If you fail to give one, or to eat one that your host or guest has given you, the Folk will give you bad luck for the entire year. I was horrified to hear of this mass consumption, enforced by the Folk, until I learned that the mince pies in question are no larger than a typical cookie. With the right recipe, an unkind practical joke on the part of the Folk becomes an excuse for indulgence.

The ancient Saxons honored Father Time, King Frost, and King Winter, who are the ancestors of Father Christmas. Each household chose a person to represent this figure, and brought him into the home. There he was crowned and treated with honor. The hospitality shown to this person demonstrated to the Folk the treatment they could expect themselves. The people believed that, if they treated his representative well, Winter himself would be kind to them.

Norse customs and beliefs, brought by the Vikings, also influenced British practices. Jul, from which the word "Yule" derives, was the midwinter persona of Odin, foremost character in the Norse pantheon. In December, Odin came to earth, visited people in secret, and gave bread to the poor. Odin, called Wotan in Britain, also led the Wild Hunt, in which a band of dead warriors flew through the sky on the night of the winter solstice. Odin was omniscient; Santa Claus knows who has been naughty or nice. In the same manner that, in Santería, African gods have taken on the names of Christian saints in order to allow their devotees to worship safely in a predominantly Christian country, so has Odin taken the alias of Santa Claus to give his adherents safe harbor in a hostile time.

Every day in Advent, the four-week period before Christmas, Britons started their main meal with a honey-sweetened cereal resembling farina. This was also a survival from Viking times. In the far north, fish and game were abundant. Grain was scarce, so grains became symbolic of wealth, abundance, and good living. In Scotland, where the climate and soil were unsuitable for wheat, they mixed oats and honey with whiskey to make Athol Brose, their characteristic midwinter drink. As a treat for the Folk, leave them a taste of Athol Brose near the fireplace on Christmas Eve, along with the usual cookies and milk.

In England in the mid-twentieth century, Santa was assisted by the Christmas Fairy. Santa's workshop was in an ice cave, accessible from English department stores.

The Irish fix up their homes in December, not only cleaning, but painting and redecorating, if they like. They decorate their homes with evergreen boughs and garlands, but not before December 24. To do so would bring bad luck. "Bringing home the Christmas" is an event to which the whole family looks forward. All the luxury shopping, the purchasing of gifts, candy, liquor, and special foods, takes place on one day.

Extended families gather. People leave lighted candles in the windows, to guide late arrivals, who may include dead ancestors and the Fair Folk. They keep a buffet set up at all times, for all visitors, natural and supernatural. They play seasonal music, and carol from house to house. The party lasts for five days, with horse racing and sporting events during the day. At night, they indulge in dancing, feasting, and storytelling. The Fair Folk of Ireland are especially fond of tall tales. Let your imagination run.

Christmas dinner consists of ham and turkey, potatoes roasted and boiled, with a trifle for dessert. Later in the evening, they will eat fruitcake and plum pudding. In a prosperous year, the main course will be roast goose; in a poor one, boiled bacon. This is better than it sounds, as Irish bacon, like Canadian bacon, is a lean, tender cured pork loin.

Irish families leave the front door unlocked when they go to bed on Christmas Eve. They leave the table set for three, and water by the window, for the convenience of supernatural visitors. They believe that the water left out will have healing properties, afterward.

They also believe that animals can talk on Christmas Eve, but that to listen in would be unlucky. Irish parents tell their children that snow on Christmas Eve means the angels are plucking the geese for their own Christmas dinners. They believe that a new moon is lucky, as is a cold night. A cold night on Christmas Eve will bring a mild spring, with no illness in the family. The Folk are expected to enter, via the unlocked door, and help themselves to the buffet. If they also wish to participate in the music and storytelling, they are welcome. Do not accept food offered by the Folk, however. Those who eat fairy food must remain in Faerie, whether they want to or not.

Like the Irish, the Scots believe that a cold Christmas is lucky, while a warm Christmas will bring poverty. They serve many kinds of cookies at Christmas. The main dish at Christmas dinner is likely to be venison stew. Scots set Christmas aside for religious observances, and keep the intense partying for Hogmany, or New Year.

In Wales, unmarried women make treacle toffee on Christmas Eve. When they test the toffee for doneness by dropping the hot syrup into cold water, the Fair Folk form the syrup into the initials of their future husbands.

The Welsh decorate abandoned coal mines as Santa's Cave. No other elf has as many homes as Santa. Instead of a Midnight Mass, common throughout Europe on Christmas Eve, Wales celebrates a Cockcrow Mass on Christmas Day at sunrise.

In earlier days, groups of masked men in Wales went from house to house with the Grey Mare. This was a horse's skull on a pole, operated as a puppet. The men asked riddles of the householders. If a householder could not solve the riddle and ask a better one, he had to give food and drink to the maskers. Early in the evening, these visits were entertaining. Later, as the men had more to drink, they became annoying, and then frightening. Eventually, the practice died out. Similar practices survived in Norway until recently. This hints that, wherever they began, they were spread by Vikings.

The maskers are impersonating the antics of the Folk, who are amusing if they are treated kindly, and dangerous if they are not. The householders are wise to the deception, but play along as long as it is fun. When the teasing turns to threats, the game is over. The Folk resent the maskers, when events turn sour. In the first place, the maskers are getting the beer and sandwiches intended for the Folk. In the second, they are giving the Folk a bad name by their misbehavior. Remember that the Folk are the dispensers of luck. A night in jail on a charge of "drunk and disorderly" could certainly be construed as bad luck.

If you maintain good humor, drink only moderately, and share the spoils with the Folk, a game of puppets and riddles would be just the thing to lure the mischievous Folk into playing with you. Be careful, though. If in doubt about the mood of your playmates, let them win.

Another Welsh tradition, still practiced, is that of the Calenigg. Children put apples on twig legs, and sell them for a few cents, or trade them for something sweet. They bring good luck to the purchaser, until the Calenigg falls apart. The children, in making lucky charms, are imitating fairy magic. The Folk show their approval by granting the magic promised by the children. The Folk, being ancient, tend to regard children with grandparently affection.

On the day after Christmas, known as Boxing Day, it is traditional in Britain to give presents to service personnel, such as letter carriers and delivery people. In the Bahamas, they have a parade similar to Mardi Gras. This is a survival, in a distant time and place, of the Feast of Fools, heir to Saturnalia. Among African-Americans, it is considered lucky to eat sweet potato pie on Boxing Day. As far as I am concerned, it is lucky to eat sweet potato pie any day.

Central Europe

In Germany, St. Nikolaus leaves small presents in children's shoes on December 6. If they have been good, the children can expect candy. If they have not, they will find twigs in their shoes instead. On Christmas Eve, adults decorate the Christmas tree with cookies, candies, and red candles, while another adult distracts the children in another room. When they bring the children in, they tell the children that an angel brought the tree, and the gifts. Germans divide Christmas Day between church and family, then spend December 26 partying with friends. The Folk spend the winter indoors, sheltering in the seasonal decorations.

As with many holidays, we find German traditions familiar because our American Christmas practices arrived with German settlers in the early days. A friend of mine, a German immigrant eager to teach me her traditions, was shocked that I already knew her secret family cookie recipe. I was just as surprised to learn that it had not originated here, since I had learned it in junior high.

German monks invented gingerbread as a way to use surplus honey. Because they raised bees in large numbers to supply the beeswax candles used in church, the monasteries always had more honey than they could use. It is also interesting to note that because honeybees provide candlewax, and candle flames represent the sun, the bees themselves are considered by some cultures to be magical emissaries between earth and heaven.

Gingerbread was used as a high-calorie energy source for eating on the road, much as we use trail mix or granola bars today. The elaborate gingerbread houses that say "Christmas" so eloquently were brought here by German immigrants, and developed into an art form. If they are left up for the duration of the holidays, they can provide both food and shelter for the Folk wintering indoors.

In addition to many kinds of baked sweets, a German Christmas feast will include venison, pork, or goose. Oddly, they only serve pork if the weather is already very cold. I say "oddly" because pork is the mainstay of the Christmas feast in the Caribbean, where it never gets as cold as the warmest Christmas in Germany. This came about because, in Germany, each family slaughtered its own pig. Before refrigeration, excess pork would spoil unless hard winter had arrived, so any meat not needed for the holiday feast was cured, and kept in the smokehouse until needed. In the Caribbean, only one pig is slaughtered in each neighborhood. The meat is used up in two days of nonstop feasting.

While Santa typically rides a sleigh pulled by eight reindeer in the United States, in Germany he may ride a white horse, a reindeer, a mule, or a goat. It is worth noting that the Norse gods also rode goatback in legend. In the far north, white animals are believed to be the property of the Folk. White reindeer, especially, are sacred.

Until recently, Germans believed that, on the Twelve Nights of Christmas, ghosts appeared, and dead warriors rode through the night sky. This is related to the Wild Hunt of British legend. Only a small step is needed for ghostly riders to become elven ones. Instead of hunting souls, our riders deliver gifts.

One of the reasons to bring a live tree into the house was to give the wood sprites, who inhabited the tree, a warm place to spend the winter. People hung bells on the limbs of the tree. When the bells rang without explanation, it meant that someone was in the tree. The candy and cookies on the tree were there for the wood sprites' nourishment.

Transylvanians, along with many Central and Eastern Europeans, eat sausage for Christmas, and many kinds of baked sweets. Hungarians round out the menu with herring, mashed potatoes, vegetables, gelatin molds, several kinds of strudel, and many kinds of cookies. They spend as much as six weeks making these cookies. The Folk are passionate about baked goods and sweets. As these are more abundant at Christmas than at any other time, the Folk are more likely to come indoors and visit with us.

Many Central and Eastern Europeans who have an orchard practice another popular custom around this time. At some point during the season, the husband will interrupt his wife while she is baking. Without allowing her time to wash her hands, he will take her to the orchard. There he will threaten each tree in turn, saying that it is worthless, and deserves to be cut down. She blocks each mock attempt at cutting down the trees, saying that she is sure that the tree will be as full of fruit as her hands are full of dough. This is less to threaten the sprites who animate the trees than to convince them of the woman's faith in the trees' fertility. The farmers hope that the Folk will continue to be generous.

The Poles perform the same ritual. There are many other Polish folk beliefs about Christmas. There is a proverb, "As goes Christmas Eve, so goes the year." For this reason, people make special efforts to be kind, gracious, and forgiving on Christmas Eve. For unmarried women who want to get married soon, the tradition is to grind poppy seeds on Christmas Eve. After dinner, they leave the house to go for a walk. They believe that their future husbands will come from the same direction from which they first hear a barking dog.

Snow at Christmas foretells an early spring. Women clean their houses thoroughly, to rid them of evil influences. As everywhere, the Folk in Eastern Europe are fanatic about cleanliness. People eat as much as they can hold, believing that the more they eat on Christmas Eve, the happier they will be all year.

While many Europeans eat preserved fish on Christmas Eve, Czechs eat their carp fresh. In fact, they buy the fish alive, and keep them in their bathtubs until they are ready to cook them.

THE FAR NORTH

In the far north, near and above the Arctic Circle, the winter solstice is a matter of urgent concern. In Rome, the weather turns from hot to mild, and the sun sets a bit earlier-ho hum. In central Europe, the weather turns from mild to cold, and the sun sets in the early afternoon. Above the Arctic Circle, the sun fails to rise at all on the winter solstice, which must surely portend cosmic disaster.

In Finland, the Christmas Goat, Jouluppukki, brings the presents. Prior to the nineteenth century, men dressed as goats roamed the streets on midwinter night, scaring children, telling dirty jokes, and begging for beer. In the nineteenth century, goat figures began to bring gifts to the children of the urban upper classes. By the twentieth century, Jouluppukki brought toys to all good Finnish children, and looked and dressed as Santa does everywhere. In fact, any Finn can tell you that Santa lives in Finnish Sapmi. They will explain, quite rationally, that he could not have his workshop at the North Pole. There is nothing at the North Pole for the reindeer to eat.

Sapmi is the land of the Sami, the original human inhabitants of northern Scandinavia and the northwestern corner of Russia. Tens of thousands of Sami continue to live in Sapmi. Many of them continue to make their living by herding reindeer. They are the model for the American mental image of Santa's elves. They wear brightly colored clothing, tasseled hats, and pointed boots that curl up at the tips. The Sami are entirely human and mortal.

While they are predominantly Lutheran at present, they hold on to their tradition of the Reindeer Fairy. Originally a human woman, she married a supernatural reindeer and gave birth to the ancestors of the Sami people. Having lived an extraordinary life, she became the Reindeer Fairy, with control over the fertility of the herds and the prosperity of the people. To gain her favor, serve red meat to your guests. She considers serving fish or vegetarian entrees to demonstrate a miserly character. (She has not, apparently, checked the price of salmon lately.) In addition, you must keep your home clean and odor-free. This does not represent mere fastidiousness on the part of the Reindeer Fairy. She and her husband lose their magical powers when they are exposed to foul odors.

Do not confuse the Reindeer Fairy with the Reindeer Elf. The Reindeer Elf is a small, hairy man who lives outdoors. He protects domestic reindeer from predators, and drives wild reindeer toward hunters. Like the Reindeer Fairy, he is entirely beneficial to human beings. As do all friendly Folk, he appreciates regular gifts of cookies and milk.

The Reindeer himself, the husband of the Reindeer Fairy, has golden antlers. He simultaneously represents the rainbow, the rain, the sun, and the entire universe. His cult is not limited to Sapmi. Figures of flying reindeer have been found all across northern Europe and Asia. To show appreciation, decorate your home with figures of flying reindeer. Gild the antlers of one. By this, he will know that you are honoring him specifically, and not just following a cultural habit by rote.

On Christmas Eve in Finland, people light candles on family graves at dusk. After that, they have a nice sauna together, followed by a personal visit from Jouluppukki. The family eats a festive dinner, consisting largely of foods that would not appeal to Americans. After dinner, the children get to open Jouluppukki's presents.

The main dish at Christmas dinner in Finland may be mutton soup, smoked mutton, lutefisk, or ham. Lutefisk is dried fish, rehydrated and soaked in lye. It was a staple food in the far north prior to refrigeration, but is eaten now only for purposes of extreme nostalgia. Rutabaga casserole is a common side dish. More appealing are the rice pudding, fruit soup, and molasses bread that typically end the meal.

In olden days in Iceland, the menu on Christmas Eve consisted of mutton soup for the prosperous, and rock ptarmigan for the poor. Now it is more likely to be leg of lamb for the middle classes, and rock ptarmigan for the rich. Smoked mutton is another Christmas delicacy unavailable in this country.

The staple diet in premodern Iceland was dried fish. All grain was imported, and expensive. It is from this shortage of grain in northern Europe that the Folk gained their lust for breads, cakes, and cookies. Cookies, cakes, and puddings were treats for special occasions, and special guests. Since Christmas was the most special day of all, Icelandic women made at least twenty kinds of pastry to celebrate it.

No evergreen trees are native to Iceland, so the old custom was to make a tree out of wood, paint it green, and decorate it with bags of candy. Now, locally grown, farmed Christmas trees are common. These are set up and decorated on December 23.

Before the Reformation, Iceland celebrated Christmas with big public parties, featuring food, drink, dancing, games, and sports. Since the Reformation, people spend more time in church. The Elves continue the parties without them, dancing in the empty houses while the inhabitants are away at church.

Even the poorest child could count on receiving a candle and a deck of cards for Christmas. However, their elders considered it unlucky to play cards on Christmas. Books were a frequent gift, for adults as well as for children. Books of folk tales and fairy stories help continue the friendly relations between the Folk and human beings.

The most important gift, for all Icelanders, was a piece of new clothing. New clothing was essential, even if it was only a pair of socks or a knit cap. At midwinter, the Yule Cat stalked through the empty streets, looking for victims. It pounced on, and devoured, anyone who was not wearing new clothing. In this case, the tradition was not put into place to court a supernatural being, but to avoid one.

Several supernatural beings everyone wants to know are the Yuletide Lads. These mischievous sprites, with names such as Door Slammer, Sausage Snatcher, and Pot Licker, are the sons of two giants who live in the mountains. The giants of the far north are evil creatures, famous for eating people and brewing bad beer. If they bother you, offer them good beer and a meal of chicken. They will go away and leave you alone.

The Lads are much nicer than their parents. While they beg food and indulge in similar forms of mild naughtiness, they distribute toys and fruit to well-behaved children. To naughty children, they give potatoes. The Lads leave these gifts in children's shoes daily, from December 12 until Christmas, when they return to the mountains. Sometimes the Lads are pictured in everyday Icelandic clothing, but sometimes they wear red suits, like Santa.

In Estonia, children put up their stockings a month before Christmas. Every day, the Elves put in sweets, toys, or books. The family puts up the tree and decorates the house on December 20. On Christmas Eve, they have a big dinner of fried goose with apples. Some families substitute chicken or turkey for the goose. The children have to sing a song or recite a poem before they get their presents. Later, there are fireworks. Adolescents play that famous old Russian game, Spin the Bottle. I wonder where that game really came from? The random kissing involved echoes fairy fertility rites.

In Denmark, people believe that if a visitor during the winter holidays leaves the home without eating, that person will take the Christmas Spirit away with him. The household Folk will defect, and follow the guest to his home. To prevent this catastrophe, each household keeps a stock of tiny cookies, too small to be refused on dietary grounds.

In Sweden, the Christmas season begins on Lucia Day, December 13, and lasts until January 13. On the morning of Lucia Day, the oldest daughter in the family dresses in white, wears a crown of leaves and lighted candles, and serves breakfast to her family. To some, this Lucia represents the fourth-century Italian saint. To others, she is a legendary Swedish heroine who distributed food to the starving during a time of famine. To still others, Lucia is a personification of light itself, so precious during the northern winter. The name Lucia means "light."

Every Swedish household has a *tomte*, an elf who protects the house, livestock, and family from harm. In order to keep the *tomte* happy, they leave a bowl of rice pudding on the doorstep for him, around Christmastime. Similarly, Norwegians leave a bowl of wheat porridge on the steps for the *Nisses* to keep them from mischief.

Some Norwegians consider Elves just another ethnic group, like Finns or Danes. Some proudly trace Elvish branches in their family trees. They will show you the borders of Elfland on a map of Norway. These same people describe the Yule customs of the Elves in ways I cannot repeat in this book, without risking censorship. If you are curious, read the *Eddas*.

Latin America

Most of Mexico takes a two-week vacation in late December, in order to celebrate Christmas in proper style. They nightly stage *Posadas*, pageants in which Mary and Joseph ask for lodgings, and are refused. After the *Posada*, there is a party.

All the women of the extended family get together before Christmas to make tamales, which are as labor-intensive as they are delicious. They exchange them with other families, in order to take advantage of a variety of recipes.

Some regions, on December 23, celebrate the Night of the Radishes. For this, people compete in creating astonishing tableaux out of carved radishes-radish villages, complete down to the chickens scratching at the roadsides. These miniature landscapes are fascinating, and beloved of the Folk.

Christmas Eve is known as *Nochebuena*, literally, "Good Night." *Nochebuena* features parades with floats, music, dancing, prizes, and fireworks. Add a good dinner and a night of romance, and you have a list of most of the human activities guaranteed to engage the interest of the Folk.

Traditionally, Mexicans did not exchange gifts until January 6, but under the influence of the United States, more and more families exchange gifts on December 25. Of course, most children prefer to receive gifts on both dates. Santa brings gifts on Christmas, while the Three Kings perform the honors on January 6.

In Cuba, the family feast takes on the character of a block party. On December 23, someone kills a pig and sets up a big barbecue. While dinner will not be ready until the next day, the beginning of the food preparation is the beginning of the party. All the neighbors drop by in turn, to help turn the spit, and bring contributions of food and drink. The big feed takes place on the twenty-fourth, when black beans, rice, and a variety of side dishes join the roast pig.

On Christmas Day, people eat leftover pork, along with a newly-cooked turkey and plenty of rice and beans. They have a decorated tree and colored lights, but the gifts wait until January 6.

In Puerto Rico the menu is similar, but everyone puts on a straw hat and pretends to be from the country. They wake up their friends by serenading them with secular holiday songs. Each successive one woken joins the revelers to wake the next. The big pig roast can take place any time between

December 16 and January 6. Instead of the Cuban black beans and *yuca con mojo,* a root vegetable with garlic sauce, side dishes are likely to be *pasteles,* which are similar to tamales, and *platanos,* which are the oversized starchy bananas that are a staple of Caribbean cuisine. Coconut makes its appearance in *tembleque,* a pudding, and coquito, a kind of eggnog.

The native Folk of the Caribbean, the ciguapas, used to live openly. They went into hiding after the Spanish conquest, out of fear that the Spaniards would force them to work in the sugar-cane fields. They look like human beings, with black hair and black or tan skin, but with their feet turned backwards. They currently live in otherwise unpopulated hill country, and under the banks of rivers. They leave their hiding places at night to look for food. There are modern accounts of ciguapas joining people in their picnic dinners. To attract ciguapas, cook outdoors, after sunset, in a place where they can smell the food cooking. Share your dinner with them, treat them kindly, and do not grow sugar cane in your yard.

Traditional families explain to their children that Santa cannot come to Puerto Rico because it is too hot for him, dressed as he is in a wool suit and fur. The children have to wait for Los Reyes Magos, the Wise Kings, who will bring their presents on January 6. More Americanized families give up and have Santa deliver after the children go to bed on Christmas Eve, as in the States.

A Spanish custom that is worth reviving is to put the names of everyone at the Christmas party in a bowl. Draw them out two by two. Each pair of people whose names are drawn together will be fast friends throughout the coming year. The Folk approve loyalty and friendship, always.

EGYPT

Even without a fierce, giant cat as incentive, everyone in Egypt gets new clothes for Christmas. If someone is too poor to obtain new clothes, charities will provide them. The Coptic Church celebrates Christmas on a different date than in the West, approximately when the West celebrates Three Kings Day. Adults are obligated to fast before Christmas, so women recruit children to taste the mountains of sweets they prepare for the feast. In this, the children are standing in for the Folk. (Fortunately, the Folk do not mind children eating their sweets for them.) The people break their fast on Christmas morning with pancakes, sweets, and milk. Since the weather is usually good, people have picnics and play outdoor sports, such as soccer and volleyball. Christmas is a popular day for weddings in Egypt. There are fireworks. Since the day features a large meal after a strict fast, indigestion is also a feature of Christmas day.

THE SOUTHERN HEMISPHERE

In Australia and New Zealand, Santa wears his red suit and fur, in spite of the heat. The reindeer get a break, though, as a team of kangaroos pulls Santa's sleigh over Australia.

Christmas falls early in the summer in Australia, shortly after the children get out of school for summer vacation. While some families have a big dinner, as in Britain or America, others sensibly defer to the heat. They have a barbecue, or a picnic of cold cuts and salad. In Australia, plum pudding is de rigueur, in spite of the weather. Little information about the native Folk of Australia is available, as the people there keep their stories secret. Among the stories that have been shared is that of the Swan Maidens. These are beautiful young women with birds' wings. They like human men, and are willing to marry them. To find Swan Maidens, go to remote pools at dawn, while they are bathing.

In New Zealand, some families cook Christmas dinner Maori style. The Maori tell stories of the Folk of their land, predating European contact. The Folk of New Zealand are blond, with light-colored skins. They are cheerful, constantly singing or giggling, and naïve. In the early days, they gave the Maori the secret of making fishnets. They like jade jewelry, and you can gain their favor by offering them some. Doing so costs nothing, as they take the shadow only, and leave the substance behind. They vanish at daybreak, so have your cookout at night if you want these Folk to join you.

To cook a pig Maori style, line a pit with hot rocks, and use retained heat to cook, as in a luau or clambake. This method of cooking takes experience. As with a Caribbean-style spit-roasted pig, it is better to hire an expert the first time. He will teach you how to do it yourself, if you ask nicely. Almost any meat can serve as the main course, accompanied by a wide variety of vegetables. The mandatory dessert is Pavlova, which is a light concoction of meringue and fresh fruit, and therefore perfectly suited to warm-weather dining.

CANADA AND THE UNITED STATES

We in the United States tend to take Canada for granted. It is a near neighbor, friendly, and, in some regions, English-speaking. A closer look, however, reveals much that is unfamiliar. For instance, it is the only country I have found that still celebrates the Festival of Madmen, the Feast of Fools, at midwinter. Different communities celebrate it on different days. Whether it is December 25, January 1, or January 6, it is a direct descendant of Saturnalia, and a prime opportunity to mingle with the Folk.

In some Canadian communities, Christkindle, an angel, and Hans Trapp, an ogre, travel together on Christmas Eve. Christkindle gives presents to well-behaved children. Hans Trapp stuffs the naughty ones into his sack and carries them off.

In other neighborhoods, Tante Arte, who is half fairy and half witch, comes down from the mountains on Christmas Eve. Riding a donkey, she gives gifts to the good children, and dunce caps to the others.

Some Canadians get their presents from Jouluppukki, who flies over directly from northern Europe.

English-speaking Canadians feast on roast goose, mince pies, plum pudding, and fruitcake. The Folk, like their hosts, prefer traditional fare on the holidays. They wash it all down with beer, ale, porter, or spiked fruit punch. French-speaking Canadians eat turkey, and follow it with imported wines. They derive the custom of eating thirteen desserts from Provence. To gain the favor of the Folk, they must taste each one. Fortunately, most of the desserts offered are small and light: dried fruits, nuts, fresh fruit, dainty cookies and cakes. They have a family supper, *Reveillon*, after Midnight Mass on Christmas Eve. They believe that the dead return to their old homes when the clock strikes midnight, but remain only until the clock finishes striking. They watch their children carefully, as the children are susceptible to the evil eye at this time.

Canadians believe that the weather on each of the Twelve Days of Christmas corresponds to the weather in each of the coming twelve months. For example, if it is clear and cold on Christmas Day, it will be clear and cold in January. This correlation is a gift of the Folk, for our convenience in planning the coming year.

If a girl wants to know the initial of her future husband, she can pour molten lead through a key ring into a pan of cold water. The Folk will form his initial in the lead. While this resembles the Welsh method of toffee divination, it is less enjoyable in that there is no toffee involved.

Another way to discover the initial of a future spouse is to carefully peel an apple, keeping the peel in one piece. Drop the apple peel onto the floor from above your head. The Folk will form it into your future spouse's initial.

Finally, to know the wishes of your heart, set a bowl of water on the windowsill in your room. You will find your inmost desires written in the frost. (I think that if water froze inside my windows, my most fervent wish would be for double-glazed windows.)

American Yule traditions are an amalgam of all the preceding ones. We give fruitcakes as gifts, but rarely eat them. Parties can take place any time between Thanksgiving and Christmas, but are considered most legitimate in late December. Christmas dinner is less elaborate than Thanksgiving, but contains many of the same dishes. Dinner is secondary in importance to the gift exchange. We court Santa and his elves with cookies and milk. If you want to stand out in his favor, add sandwiches and coffee to Santa's offering. He has a long night ahead of him, and northerners like their coffee.

While it has become usual in the United States to go into debt to buy extravagant Christmas presents, I have to advise against the practice. The Folk do not respect irresponsibility, and are likely to withdraw their favor from the improvident. Instead of spending a lot of money, spend your time making thoughtful gifts for your loved ones.

Many use Yule as a reason to give the grandest party of the year. I am among them. I invite almost everyone I know, and invite them to bring along their friends and relatives as well. Everyone who crosses my threshold on the night of the party gets a present, even if it is an inexpensive trinket. There is plenty of food. Generally, I shop for this one party all year, wrap presents for two or three days, and spend another two days cooking. If my husband did not pitch in with the cleaning, I would have to allow another two days for that.

It is important to treat everyone who enters your home with kindness and generosity, as you do not know who strangers may be. Gods as diverse as Loki and Zeus have paid incognito visits to their people. In the Christian tradition, Jesus is recorded as having recommended kindness to strangers, saying, "What you have done to these...you have done to me."

As all the parties are packed into a few short weeks, most people have only the time and strength to attend two or three. There are other ways to express hospitality that are less taxing. Cookie exchanges, initiated in the last couple of decades, fit in well with modern life. Almost no one has the time any more to make the great variety of cookies that were the norm two or three generations ago. In order to correct this deficiency, people make large numbers of one or two kinds of cookies, and exchange with others who have done the same. Make plenty, in case there are unexpected guests, natural or supernatural. Remember what happened to Sleeping Beauty, all because her parents did not have enough to go around.

MISTLETOE

I have not mentioned the mistletoe traditions of various lands, preferring to treat them together.

In the Norse myths, the dart that killed Balder, the most beloved of the gods, was made of mistletoe. Balder's mother wished to extract an oath from everything on earth not to harm her son, but she neglected to get the oath from the mistletoe, as it seemed insignificant. Nor was it an enemy who threw it at him, but a friend who tossed it as a joke. Many lessons can be derived from this, among them the inevitability of death, and the importance of avoiding hubris. It is essential to adopt a modest attitude when dealing with the supernatural.

The importance of mistletoe to the Celts was as an evergreen associated with deciduous trees. While its host became barren, it remained green. It was the Golden Bough, emblematic of immortality.

The use of mistletoe as a charm during the midwinter holidays has come down without interruption, but with some variations. Until recently, a kiss under the mistletoe in France has been tantamount to a proposal of marriage. Under Druid rule, a kiss under the mistletoe was an unbreakable pledge of friendship, equivalent to signing a treaty.

In the United States, mistletoe gives license to kiss, a mild echo of the sexual license available during Saturnalia. Regardless of marital status, one may kiss whomever one likes, as long as the meeting takes place under the mistletoe. If you hear giggling when you kiss, do not look for the source. It is the Folk, spying on you.

TRADITIONAL HOLIDAY FARE

FRUITCAKE

Americans take it for granted that fruitcakes are to be seen, and not eaten. We think of them as being useful only as doorstops, or as gifts for less-favored relatives. I used to think about fruitcake that way, too. Then I faced annual requests for fruitcake from a favorite friend, and realized that I would have to learn to make them.

Supermarket fruitcakes taste nasty. If you want one that is suitable for use as food, you have only two choices. You can send large amounts of money to a specialty baker, or you can make the fruitcakes yourself. This is not inexpensive, either. On the other hand, the time and expense invested in fruitcake will set you apart from the crowd, and please everyone on your gift list who likes fruitcake. Both of them.

The way to make fruitcake taste good is to put only things that taste good in it. If this were self-evident, no one would buy those little plastic buckets labeled "Fruitcake Mix." Only buy fruits you like, in identifiable packages. If you are not tempted to snag a bite or two while you are cooking, it does not belong in your fruitcake. I recommend candied cherries and pineapple, complemented by dried fruits: golden raisins, dates, apricots. Add any nuts you like: pecans, walnuts, almonds, hazelnuts, macadamias. If some of the fruits and nuts are homegrown, the magic is doubled. If you want to use candied citrus peel, make your own, unless you really want the toxic bite that commercial peel provides.

What follows is my recipe for Jazz Fruitcake, so called because improvisation is key. I have made it every year for more than a decade, but never the same way twice. It varies according to what I have on hand, what has come out of my garden, what is available at the market, and what I am in the mood for.

One thing I never vary is the liquor, but you may. As a matter of ethnic pride, I always use a dark Puerto Rican rum. You, of course, may use any high-test alcohol you prefer. One of the reasons for my fruitcake's popularity is the ignorance with which I first approached it. After the cakes are baked and cooled, I pour a pint or more of rum over the tops of all of them. It was years before I found out that, classically, a fruitcake should be dressed with only an ounce or so of liquor. My way is better.

JAZZ FRUITCAKE

Makes 3 loaves

4 cups flour

1 tsp baking powder

4 tsp nutmeg

1 cup butter

2 cups granulated sugar

6 eggs

½ cup liquor (rum, brandy, or whiskey)

4 cups any kind of nuts

1 pound any dried fruit

1 pound any candied fruit

1 ½ cups additional liquor

Stir first three ingredients together, and set aside. Cream butter and sugar together until fluffy. Beat in eggs, one at a time. Add dry ingredients, alternating with liquor. Stir in fruits and nuts. Turn into three well-greased 9-inch by 5-inch loaf pans. Bake at 300º until browned, and test for doneness: approximately 1 hour, 15 minutes. Let cool in pan for 15 minutes, then turn onto wire rack to cool completely. When *completely* cool, place in airtight containers, pour ½ cup additional liquor over each cake, seal, and allow to rest for at least one month. Check iden-tification when serving, and do not give to minors.

ICEBOX COOKIES

Yield varies, depending on size of cookies.

⅔ cup butter

½ cup sugar

1 egg

2 tsp vanilla extract

2 cups flour

1 tsp baking powder

½ tsp salt

½ cup chopped nuts (optional)

Cream butter with sugar, then beat in egg and vanilla. Sift together dry ingredients, and stir into butter mixture. Add nuts, if using.

Divide dough in half. If desired, add 2 Tbsp cocoa powder to one half. Form each into a log of the diameter desired for the finished cookies. Wrap in plastic and chill for several hours. You may wrap chocolate and vanilla logs together, to make cookies that are half one and half the other.

When you are ready for hot, fresh cookies, unwrap logs, slice ¼" thick, and arrange on cookie sheets that have been lightly buttered, or sprayed with nonstick coating. Bake at 325º for 15 minutes until set, and vanilla portions slightly golden.

Sharon Johnson's Julekage

Makes 1 large loaf

1 cup warm milk
½ cup granulated sugar
½ tsp salt
½ tsp ground cardamom
1 package active dry yeast
1 egg
2 Tbsp soft butter
3 ¼ cups flour, divided in half
¼ cup golden raisins
¼ cup dried, diced pineapple
¼ cup dried, diced apricots

Mix all ingredients except fruit and second half of flour. Beat well. Add remaining flour and fruit. Knead until smooth and elastic, about 10 minutes. Place in buttered bowl, and turn over to butter top. Cover and let rise in warm place until double in volume. Punch down, and let rise until doubled again. Punch down, shape into a round loaf, and put into a buttered, round cake pan. Cover and let rise until double (this could take all day). Bake at 350º until golden brown, about 50 minutes.

ATHOL BROSE

Serves 6

This legendary potable has been around long enough for recipes to vary wildly. I have seen them all the way from whiskey barely touched with honey and oats, to whipped cream seasoned with whiskey and garnished with toasted oats. This recipe makes a liqueur comparable to Irish Cream in taste and texture, but without any dairy component.

1 cup rolled oats
1 cup water
2 Tbsp honey
1 cup good-quality Scots whiskey

Soak oats in water overnight. In the morning, squeeze soaked oats through a fine-meshed strainer to extract the starchy essence of the oat. Add honey and whiskey to oat squeezings. Let mellow a couple of days. Serve cool. May be topped with cream (it is oatmeal, after all).

HOT TODDY

Serves 1

This beverage does double-duty. It is both a festive cold-weather libation and an effective symptom-soother for winter-raw throats. Cheers!

1 cup strong, hot tea
1 Tbsp brown sugar
Juice and peel of ½ lemon
2 Tbsp dark rum

Mix it all in a heat-proof mug, and wrap your hands around it as you sip.

TREACLE TOFFEE

Makes about 1 pound

The first time I tasted this candy I did not like it. Within a few hours, I had finished the 3-ounce package that had been in my Christmas basket and phoned the donor to try to obtain a steady supply. It has an odd, and oddly addictive, taste. Now that I know how to make it, I am free of the whims of candy importers.

1 cup molasses
2 cups granulated sugar
¼ cup water
2 Tbsp butter
1 Tbsp vinegar

Combine all ingredients in a large, heavy saucepan. Cook, stirring frequently, until syrup dropped into ice water forms a very hard mass. Test it by chewing a bit. When it feels as if it could almost pull the fillings out of your teeth, it is ready. Pour onto a well-buttered cookie sheet to cool. When cooled, slam it onto a hard surface to break it into bite-sized pieces.

MINCEMEAT

Makes enough for one 9-inch pie, or 2-dozen cookie-sized tartlets.

Mincemeat was originally a meat dish, using small amounts of sugar, vinegar, and spices to preserve the meat. Gradually, fruits were added. The proportion of fruit to meat increased over time, until meat was eliminated from the recipe around 1970. This recipe approximates one from the late nineteenth century. It is delicious.

½ pound raw lean beef

3 apples, cored and chopped

½ cup raisins

1 cup brown sugar

3 Tbsp molasses

6 Tbsp vinegar

¼ tsp ground cloves

½ tsp ground allspice

¼ tsp salt

1 tsp cinnamon

¼ cup liquor (rum, brandy, or whiskey)

Grind meat, apples, and raisins. Mix in nonreactive pan and add remainder of ingredients. Cook together over medium-low heat, stirring frequently, for 30 minutes, until liquid is absorbed.

To make into a pie, use any pastry recipe, or even frozen pie shells. To make tiny tartlets, roll two pieces of pastry out flat. Place teaspoonfuls of mincemeat in rows, two inches apart, on one sheet of pastry. Cover with the other sheet. Press gently with your fingers in between mincemeat bulges, to seal. Cut into individual tartlets, and bake according to pastry recipe. If you have a ravioli mold, the process will be that much simpler.

If you want a vegetarian product, substitute chopped walnuts for the beef.

ROAST PORK

Serves 4

Another dish that is both simple and delicious. I make it as often as my figure will allow. The cumin and lime make it specifically Caribbean.

1 pork shoulder roast, approximately 4 pounds
Granulated garlic
Ground black pepper
Ground cumin (optional)
Juice of 1 lime (optional)

Preheat oven to 325°. Sprinkle meat all over with garlic, pepper, and cumin. Put in nonreactive roaster. Squeeze lime over meat, if desired; cover, and bake at 325° for 3 hours.

BAKED YAMS

Serves 4

An island favorite, plain, they can be peeled and used in any recipe calling for cooked yams. I always make extra, to use in recipes over the next few days.

2 large yams

Preheat oven to 350°. Scrub yams, place on sheet pan, and bake until they yield to gentle pressure, approximately 2 hours. Serve with butter as a side dish, or with butter and cheese as a vegetarian entrée.

Black Beans

Serves 6 as an entrée, 12 as a side dish.

1 pound dry black beans
Water to cover by 2 inches
1 can (approximately 1 pound, 14 ounces) diced tomatoes
1 large onion, diced
1 Tbsp salt
½ Tbsp ground black pepper
1 tsp red pepper flakes
1 tsp granulated garlic

Sort beans. Discard broken or moldy beans, along with any rocks or debris. Rinse. Place in large, heavy saucepan, and cover with water to cover by 2 inches. Cover and bring to boiling point over medium heat. Reduce heat and simmer until beans are very tender, 2 to 3 hours. Check frequently to be sure that beans remain covered with water. Add more boiling water if necessary.

When beans are tender, add remaining ingredients, adjusting seasonings to taste. Simmer 30 minutes more, and serve with white rice or corn tortillas.

Rice for a Crowd

Steaming rice in salted water on top of the stove works for up to 2 cups of uncooked rice, but not for large quantities. If you want to make large amounts of rice for a big party, use this oven technique.

For each 12 servings, put 3 cups of long-grain rice in a baking pan with ½ cup butter. Place in 350° oven to melt butter and toast rice slightly. For each 3 cups of rice, bring 6 cups of water to a boil with 1½ tsp of salt. When it boils, carefully pour it onto hot rice in the oven. It will spatter. Stir it once, cover, and bake for 20 minutes more.

COQUITO:
COCONUT EGGNOG

Serves 12

I like to prepare the coquito without rum, and let my guests add their own to taste.

3 cans coconut milk, *not* cream of coconut
¾ cup granulated sugar
8 beaten eggs
1 Tbsp vanilla extract
1 cup dark rum

Combine coconut milk and sugar in saucepan. Bring to boiling point and remove from heat. Slowly pour coconut milk mixture into beaten eggs, beating constantly with wire whisk. Return mixture to saucepan and stir over low heat until mixture thickens slightly. Do not boil. Strain into serving pitcher. Stir in vanilla and rum. Chill before serving.

YANKEE CHRISTMAS

Makes approximately 2 pounds.

This sweet is inspired by the Australian favorite, "White Christmas." It would not be recognized as such by an actual Aussie. "White Christmas" is made using copha, *a solidified coconut oil virtually unobtainable stateside. I substituted white chocolate, and took liberties with the fruit. That said, my version has proven wildly popular with fans of white chocolate.*

1 pound good-quality white chocolate, made with cocoa
   butter
3 cups crisped rice cereal
¼ cup golden raisins
¼ cup chopped dried apricots
¼ cup dried sweetened cranberries
1 cup shredded coconut

Melt white chocolate in a large, heavy saucepan over very low heat. Gently stir in remainder of ingredients. Spread onto plastic wrap-lined cookie sheet and allow to harden in refrigerator. Break into pieces to serve.

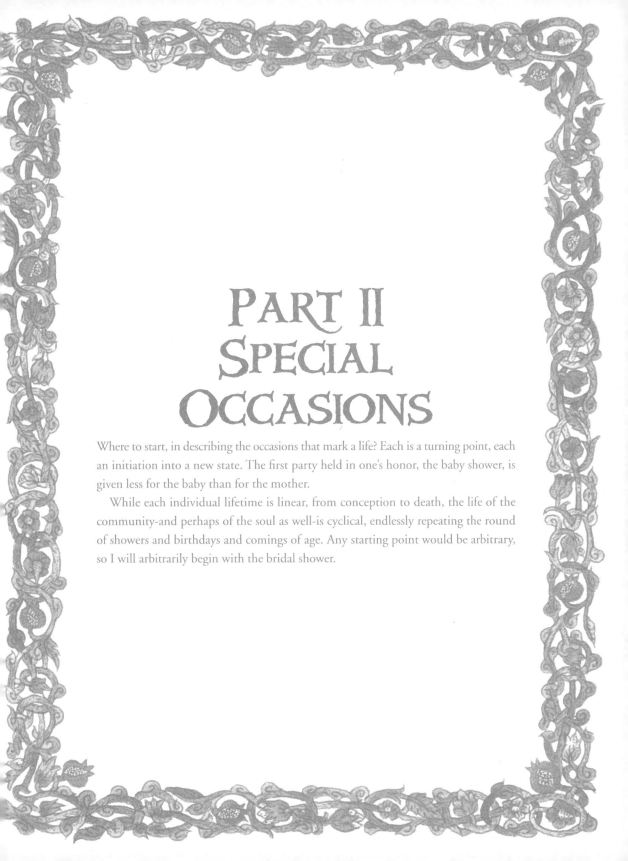

PART II
SPECIAL
OCCASIONS

Where to start, in describing the occasions that mark a life? Each is a turning point, each an initiation into a new state. The first party held in one's honor, the baby shower, is given less for the baby than for the mother.

While each individual lifetime is linear, from conception to death, the life of the community-and perhaps of the soul as well-is cyclical, endlessly repeating the round of showers and birthdays and comings of age. Any starting point would be arbitrary, so I will arbitrarily begin with the bridal shower.

CHAPTER 26
BRIDAL SHOWER

The custom of showering a bride-to-be with household goods came about as community support for a young couple in love. If the family was too poor to set the young couple up in their first home, or if the family of the bride objected to the marriage and refused to provide a dowry, the friends of the bride and groom could get together and provide the necessities of a new home.

The bride's friends should throw the shower. The bride cannot do so, for two reasons: The first, and most important, is that it is never becoming to ask for gifts for oneself. Encouraging gifts to the bride is the primary reason for a bridal shower, the assumption being that she is a sweet young thing who doesn't own so much as a skillet. The second, practical, reason is that it is impossible to be simultaneously the hostess and the guest of honor. According to the strictest etiquette, family members of the bride should not host the shower either. A shower is a substitute for a dowry. If the family is involved, and able, they should give her enough in the way of cash and dry goods to set her up in her new role as a married woman.

That said, anyone who is not the bride and not a member of her immediate family may throw her a shower. In cases where the bride belongs to more than one social circle, she may have multiple showers. For instance, her colleagues may throw her a shower during a lunch break at work, while her friends from school may throw her another on a Saturday afternoon. The bride's only responsibility is to smile and say, "Thank you." A lot.

The hostess's duties are to invite everyone who might be interested in giving a gift to the bride, and to provide a venue, refreshments, and limited entertainment. No one should be invited to the shower who has not been invited to the wedding. Doing so sends the message that the bridal couple wants their gifts, but not their blessing on the marriage itself. Alas, people who elope, or who have very small weddings, are doomed to receive very few gifts. This is often all the encouragement the couple needs to have a big wedding.

As the Fair Folk heartily endorse love matches, they enjoy and approve this kind of shower. Most of the fairy blessings lingering after the party will cling to the location where it was held. For this reason, the home where the couple will be living after the wedding is the best place for a shower. If the bridal couple does not have their home yet, the shower should be held in a place where the couple spends a lot of time, and that has happy memories associated with it. It could be the home of a friend or relative, or a nearby park or botanical garden.

Do not have the shower in a restaurant unless it can provide a private room for the party. The bride and guests will need the freedom to shriek with delight as the bride opens the gifts.

Refreshments for a bridal shower need be no more than something sweet plus something to drink, as long as the time allotted to the shower does not overlap a mealtime. If you invite people over at noon, you are honor-bound to serve them lunch, just as you must serve dinner if you invite people over at 7:00 p.m. If you invite people over for two hours beginning at 2:00 P.M., punch and cake will suffice. Have more on hand than you think you will need, for the Folk. It is bad luck to run out of food at a party.

Any book or magazine on weddings can provide dozens of ideas for games appropriate to bridal showers. Some of them might even be fun, for some people. Please limit them to two or three. Some of us find them excruciating. Do not underestimate the entertainment value of open, undirected conversation. For us older folks, nothing matches the amusement of hearing the advice young, single women give each other about marriage.

What about a coed shower? If the men in your circle are interested in such things, go ahead and invite them. If the groom runs away screaming at the mention of a shower, let him off the hook. Do whatever seems like the most fun for the people involved.

What if the mother of the bride, or the bride's sister, wants to throw a shower? No problem. Call it a reception in honor of the bride, or a tea party. As long as the word "shower" is not mentioned, she can throw any party she likes. The guests are likely to bring presents anyway, out of habit, affection for the bride, and inattention to detail. "Oh, I thought this was a *shower*!" they will say. The best part is, that none of the usual shower games are appropriate. The guests may talk, mingle, and laugh however they like.

If the hostess insists on having a theme, beyond simply "bridal shower," it should be a practical one. A kitchen shower or a linen shower is related to the business of setting up a household. A music shower or a beer shower is not.

Do not expect the Fair Folk to participate in an office-based party. The Folk who hang around office buildings tend to be computer bugs and the gremlins who cause the copier to malfunction. The Good Neighbors will be at the parties thrown in homes, attended by actual friends and relatives.

CHAPTER 27
WEDDING

My first and most important piece of advice is this: No matter who you are, no matter how experienced a cook or caterer you are, *do not cater your own wedding*. This has nothing to do with luck, custom, or the Fair Folk, but with the unique stressors involved in one's own wedding. It is said that a lawyer who represents himself may be a good lawyer, but he has a fool for a client. Similarly, a woman who caters her own wedding may be a fine caterer, but she will not be much of a bride. I tried it. While guests—my betrothed's friends and relatives, whom I had never met—filed in, I was assembling lasagna. Wearing jeans and a t-shirt, I waved a ladle over my head, chanting, "I'm the bride! I'm the bride!" My future cousins-in-law gravitated to a pretty guest who was wearing a long white dress and a lace hat, believing her to be my fiancé's intended. That was bad for my ego, and worse for the lasagna.

My second piece of advice, also born of hard experience, is this: If you choose to get married in your own home, you *must* spend your wedding night in a hotel. This is not to avoid malevolent spiritual influences, but your wedding guests. Some people would rather hang around far into the evening, congratulating you on your marriage, than get out of the way so you can consummate it. It all seems so obvious, after the fact.

Learn from my experience. Hire someone else to do the cooking, and go to a hotel.

Hard practicalities in place, how does one enlist the favor of the Folk at a wedding? Make them feel welcome. Have the wedding outdoors, or in a pri-

vate home. Rope off a few chairs, to save a place for them. If you need to jus-
tify this, tell whoever asks that you are saving a place for Aunt Flora, who
may arrive late. Have a few extra plates, and plenty of food and drink. Put a
piece of wedding cake aside for the Folk. You can leave it outside after the
wedding—unless it's chocolate, which is yummy for us, but toxic to some
other species. If your wedding cake is chocolate, leave alternate pastries or
cookies for the benefit of nonhuman guests.

It is not necessary to spend great amounts of money on a wedding in order
to favorably impress the Folk. Many families spend the equivalent of the
down payment on a house, or a year's tuition at an Ivy League university, on
a wedding. That money would be better spent on, say, a down payment on
a house or a year's tuition at an Ivy League university. For all the talk of "fairy
princesses," the Folk are, on the whole, a blue-collar lot. The leprechauns are
shoemakers; the knockers are coal miners. They are not impressed by rented
mansions, vintage champagne, and designer gowns. The bride's mother's
garden is a more suitable place for a wedding than a grand manor, if the
manor in question is not actually the bride's childhood home. If the invited
guests will not fit into the host's home, public parks and their recreation
rooms are available for a reasonable fee.

A church is a good place for the ceremony *only* if the bride or the groom
actually belongs to that church. To use a consecrated spot solely for its aesthetic value smacks faintly of sacrilege. In addition, some sects are openly
hostile to the Folk, calling them demons. If the bridal couple wants a beautiful stone building, but does not belong to a church that owns the sort of
building they have in mind, they have other options available. Look into
public buildings. Libraries and museums have meeting rooms and galleries that
can be rented for private parties. Botanical gardens and historical museums
have some of the best. Remember that the blessing of the Fair Folk clings to
the location. You will best obtain the lasting benefit of their participation in
your wedding if you hold it in a place you frequent.

If you like them, and can easily afford them, go ahead and have a fleet of
limousines and a river of champagne. Be aware, however, that they will do
nothing to increase your stature with the Folk. They will be more impressed
by a gown made by the bride, or made as a gift of love by her best friend,
than by one from the finest atelier in Paris.

CHAPTER 28
BABY SHOWER

The baby shower is not actually in honor of the baby, although the people present speak of little else. The baby shower is, in fact, a festive community anticipation of a woman's initiation into motherhood.

No other rite of passage changes a woman's life as much as new motherhood does. The transitions from student to professional, or from single woman to married woman, are child's play compared to the transition from childless woman to mother. Not only does a woman's daily routine change, along with her sleep patterns and her level of awareness, but many of her beliefs change, and most of her priorities as well. Nothing can prepare her for this metamorphosis before it happens, but the presence of a community of women can cushion the blow. The function of a baby shower is to identify this community, so the new mother can know where to turn when she needs support. Her childless friends can help, with gifts of babysitting and company. Friends who have older children, especially friends belonging to her mother's generation, can give advice and priceless been-there-done-that comfort. The transformation from chrysalis to butterfly is probably just as painful, but I have never heard the butterfly complain about it afterward.

Gifts at a baby shower are mandatory, for their symbolic value more than any other. Playsuits, bibs, and tiny dresses cost little. Their message of welcome to the infant and support to the mother is priceless. The big expenses of parenthood, which are medical insurance, a larger home, and a few pieces of sturdy furniture, will not be addressed by shower guests. That's what grandparents are for.

As with all parties, the keys to obtaining the blessing of the Folk at a baby shower are to have the party at home, preferably outdoors, and to have plenty of room and food for extra guests. Having these things will also prove useful if Aunt Helen brings her friend Jean, who is not only an obstetrical nurse, but the mother of four teenagers who love to babysit. It is good to have friends.

The hostess should prevent the guests from telling the expectant mother horror stories about labor and delivery. The mother-to-be may have an easier time of giving birth than her friends did. If she does not, no purpose will have been served by frightening her ahead of time. Better topics of discussion are baby names, and whether the baby would be prettier with her mother's nose or her father's. Planning the baby's brilliant career in medicine is also acceptable, as long as the parents realize that the career will ultimately be their child's decision, and not their own. There are, of course, myriad party games available for baby showers, as there are for bridal showers. I do not like them. Play one or two if you must, but make sure that your guests are enjoying them.

Now and for several months after the birth, the new mother's friends should be exquisitely kind to her. Between sleep deprivation and hormonal fluctuations, a new mother can easily become depressed. The Folk covet human women as nurses for their own babies. One who is depressed is at increased risk for abduction by the Folk, with dire results. See that the new mother has every reason to feel loved and supported. If you see signs of depression, such as loss of interest in her usual pleasures, urge her to get professional help.

CHAPTER 29
WELCOMING THE BABY

The baby has made her appearance, and the mother has recovered sufficiently to receive visitors. Nine days or so after the birth, if all has gone well, there should be another party.

Most religions have a ceremony specified for receiving the infant into their faith community. Whatever the ceremony, part of it often involves naming secondary parents for the infant. These people, usually called "godparents" in English, take upon themselves a serious commitment. While this responsibility is not legally enforceable, the godparents accept the moral obligation to raise the child, in the event of the deaths of the parents. This rarely takes place. In the unlikely event of the deaths of both parents, the child usually goes to live with another relative, not the godparents. Still, it is something a person should consider, before agreeing to become a godparent. Usually, the duties of a godparent are limited to giving the child presents for birthdays and coming-of-age celebrations, and being available as an adult friend to the child. An adult friend is especially valuable during and after adolescence, when children find it increasingly difficult to talk to their parents.

A lucky baby will have two parents, two godparents, four grandparents, and a motley assortment of aunts, uncles, cousins, and siblings. Any of these can host the welcoming party for the infant. Whoever of the aforementioned has the room, a convenient location, and the desire to throw a wingding, may do so. In some cultures, the welcome is an intimate affair, with just family and best friends invited. In others, there may be hundreds of guests, a live band, a few kegs of beer, and a whole barbecued steer. It all depends on the desires of the parents and grandparents. The baby will have little to say in the matter.

There is an old belief that the Folk steal babies and leave pieces of wood, or their own elderly relatives, in their stead. This unfortunate belief may have come about in response to illnesses, such as polio, that cause sudden, dramatic changes in the baby's appearance. The best protection against this type of abduction is to keep the baby's vaccinations up to date.

There are several traditional means of protecting children from abduction by the Folk. These include dressing boys as girls, under the ridiculous assumption that the Folk prefer boys. Others include putting a blue bead on a string around the infant's neck, and putting something made of iron in or near the crib. Unisex onesies are a convenient form of dress for babies, but I would question the wisdom of forcing children to cross-dress, once they are old enough to know the difference. A baby can choke on a bead, or strangle on its string. An iron ornament, firmly attached to the crib, would probably be the charm least likely to cause problems of its own. Knowing, and being on good terms with, the resident Folk is far and away the best means for securing the infant's safety.

Whatever form the welcoming party takes, one or more of the principal adults (parents, godparents, grandparents) should take the infant around the property and introduce him to his surroundings. This holds true whether the family lives in a basement apartment or a grand estate. The baby will not remember the tour, but the Folk will appreciate the courtesy. They will know from the introduction that the baby belongs there, and has come to stay.

CHAPTER 30
BIRTHDAYS

Every birthday is an initiation for a child, as a one year old is a different thing from a newborn, and a kindergartner is a different thing from a preschooler. A child's birthday party looms second only to Christmas as a landmark of the year—first, if the family does not celebrate Christmas.

It is not necessary to go to great expense for a child's birthday party. Pony rides, bounce houses, and professional clowns are not the essence of the day. What is essential is to have a few relatives, several friends, and a cake. For a child under twelve, the cake *must* have one candle for every year achieved, and it should be homemade. No bakery can add the love that a parent can put into a cake. If baking is not your forte, you need not make it from scratch. If baking is beyond you, at least decorate it yourself.

Using a media tie-in as a theme is not conducive to cementing relations with the Fair Folk. Creative activities, and activities that foster the love of nature, are. In lieu of party games, have the children transplant flowers from six-packs into small pots, which they can then take home. Give them paper and paint, or craft sticks and glue, and see what happens. Invite a neighbor to show off her exotic pets, or a hobby farmer to bring over a few barnyard animals. A rabbit, chicken, or goat will enthrall a roomful of city kids. Have the children draw faces on paper bags, and stage puppet shows with the results. If you have a concrete driveway, give them colored chalk, and permission to go wild. For older children, give them blank t-shirts, which can be obtained inexpensively at craft or discount stores, and an assortment of dyes and fabric paints. Warn their parents about this ahead of time, so the guests attend the party in their painting clothes. Face painting is fun for all ages. Adults can paint the faces of young children, while the older ones can paint each other. Face paints are available everywhere in the fall, and all year in costume shops.

Provide pizza as well as cake and ice cream, along with punch or soda, and you will be a hero. Order out for the pizza. You will be too busy supervising to cook, and pizza is cheap.

The Folk love children, and will often reveal themselves to children when they will not reveal themselves to adults. Laughter attracts them, and story-telling, and all kinds of creative play.

Beyond twelve years of age, adolescents prefer to plan their own parties, with adult participation limited to paying for everything. Have courage.

CHAPTER 31
COMING OF AGE

Once upon a time, communities staged events to accept young people into adult society. Boys were taken into the men's quarters, where they were instructed in the secrets of manhood. After passing a test of courage, they were called men, and never again treated as children. Similarly for girls, initiated into womanhood.

With only a few survivals, these rites are unknown in the U.S. The bar mitzvah and bat mitzvah, intended as initiations into adulthood, take place too early in a child's life to realistically function as such. If a thirteen year old took on an adult role, working full time to support a family, the neighbors would report that family to Child Protective Services.

Sweet Sixteen parties and debutante balls are all but extinct, and no corresponding ceremonies are available to boys ready to become men. The closest equivalent, at least on the West Coast, is getting a driver's license. More than graduating or getting that first apartment, driving a car makes a teenager feel like an adult.

The one public celebration that is still practiced, and taken seriously as the coming of age is a *quinceanera* of a fifteen-year-old girl. On the fifteenth birthday of a Latina girl, her extended family throws a huge bash, comparable to a wedding in scale.

The family reserves the local church for a religious ceremony, conducted by a priest, at which the young woman vows to conduct herself properly and to serve her community and her church. Prior to the Spanish conquest, the *quinceanera* would have given her thanks to the indigenous gods; this is a very old custom. She is attended by fourteen girls and boys her own age, who are her friends and relatives. All are formally and uniformly dressed, as the attendants at a wedding would be. After the church service, the whole party repairs to a hall for a dinner dance. In token of the *quinceanera's* new status as a grown woman, her mother puts a tiara on her head. Her father removes her flat shoes and replaces them with high heels. She gives her best doll to a younger sister, as a gesture that she no longer needs childish amusements. She dances, first with her father, then in turn with each of the men and boys present. She is no longer a child.

It is a lovely custom, but I am not sure it would work outside the culture that developed it. For one thing, I am unsure whether most American teenage boys can be induced to don a tuxedo for a formal dance. Then again, if that is where the girls are, eventually the boys will follow.

The Folk are always interested in affairs of the human heart. Parties and dances that foster romantic entanglements especially intrigue them. The *quinceanera* festivities, being the public celebration that a girl is old enough to date, would be sure to engage the attention of the Folk.

CHAPTER 32
HOUSEWARMING

The purpose of a housewarming is to metaphorically warm the new home. It is an opportunity for your friends to find out where you live, how to get there, how you are living now. It is an opportunity for you to show them that you have not left them behind with the old neighborhood. It is an opportunity to make friends with your new neighbors.

An individual or family should have a housewarming as soon as they have unpacked and decorated. Whether they plan it as such or not, the first party they have in their new home will function as a housewarming. The hosts will give their guests "the nickel tour," showing them bedrooms, workshops, closets, and other private areas that will be off-limits to guests ever after. The guests will ask questions regarding the cost of the house and the terms of the mortgage, which would be intolerably invasive at any other time. Hosts may answer vaguely, as long as they maintain good cheer.

No one expects fancy cooking or professional entertainment at a housewarming. Your friends will be suitably impressed that you have even hung your pictures on the wall. Feed them a pot of spaghetti or chili, or even a take-out pizza. It will be banquet enough. Your guests are likely to bring you small gifts to make you feel at home. The sooner you throw the party after you actually move, the more generous your friends are likely to be, and the less they will expect in the way of entertainment.

This first party will show the Folk already resident in your new location what kind of person you are. To gain their favor, you want to create the impression that you are generous, friendly, and fun to be around. This is also a chance for you to assure the Folk who accompanied you from your old home that you still value your relationship with them. The move will have upset them. Let them know that you are still the party animal they know and love. Put familiar objects on display. A few vases, houseplants, and pictures from the old house will help make the Folk feel at home. Don't replace all your furniture at once; keep some of it long enough for the Folk to feel comfortable in their new surroundings.

CHAPTER 33
RETIREMENT

A h, the retirement party. A speech, a pat on the back, an expensive catered lunch that the guests paid for themselves. It is too bad businesses do not give out gold watches any more. The friendly Folk do not attend office parties. The Folk who do, computer bugs and gremlins, you do not want to associate with. Have a real party after the office party, in your own home, with your real friends.

Make a speech there, too. At the office, your speech detailed how grateful you were to be able to work with such a splendid crew. At home, you can tell the truth. You are glad you will never again have to get up before dawn to fight traffic. You are delighted that you will never again have to spend the larger part of every day doing battle with dunderheads. Ceremonially destroy a piece of clothing that you hate, and wore only because dress code required it: a tie, or a pair of pantyhose. Announce your retirement plans, whether they include roaming the country in an RV, writing the Great American Novel, or putting your feet up and watching TV.

Let the champagne flow. You have earned it. Remember to pour out a bit on the ground, for the Folk. You are going to have a lot of time to spend with them, now.

PART III
NUTS
AND
BOLTS

I keep telling you to throw parties, but so far, I have not given much concrete direction on how that is done. This is the part where I correct that.

CHAPTER 34
THE INTIMATE DINNER PARTY

You may have already thrown dozens of these, without realizing it. Any time you call up a few friends and say, "Come on over. I'm cooking a _____," you are throwing an intimate dinner party. These can take place as often as you like, and need have no other rationale than a desire to spend a few hours with friends.

Candles, flowers, and soft music are all nice, but not necessary. All you really need, to throw a dinner party, are good food, good friends, and a place to sit.

Cook within your level of confidence. If you have never cooked anything more complicated than tuna salad, do not try to make soufflés for company. On the other hand, it is okay to try out new recipes on friends, as long as you warn them first. "Are you free for dinner Friday? I have some new recipes I want to try," has been a good opening line for me. Of course, these are recipes that are similar to ones I have made before, and I only try them out on close friends. If I were trying to impress someone, I would make one of my specialties. For my father-in-law, I make only things that I could make blindfolded in an earthquake.

How do you put together a dinner party? I call my guests first. The size of your dining-room table dictates the maximum size of your guest list for a sit-down dinner. Formal etiquette declares that the hosts determine the menu, and guests have to live with it. In practice, a good host considers the guests' needs. For a small party, it is not difficult to plan a menu that will be acceptable to your guests, taking into account allergies, religious restrictions, and other dietary needs. Even in a large group, try to have something everyone can eat.

Once you have determined the guest list and the menu, compare the contents of your pantry with the things you will need. Go to the market the day before the party. Get everything you need. If you have enough room, get ice, too. If you do not have enough room in your freezer for ice, have one of your friends pick it up on the way over. You probably will not have enough time to pick it up yourself on the day of the party.

Some dishes hold well, and can be made on the day before the party. Chili is in this category, as are most soups and stews. Other dishes must be served as soon as they are made. These are most appropriate for very small groups. If there is a large group, it will be impossible to coordinate your guests and your kitchen so that people are hungry at the exact moment the soufflés come out of the oven.

Clean house as thoroughly as possible, a day or two before the party. People will not trust the wholesomeness of the food if the kitchen is not immaculate. Put a clean cloth on the table, and set it before your guests arrive. If you do not have cats, you can set the table the day before the party. The dishes will not go anywhere.

Have something on the table to eat as soon as your guests arrive, in case they are famished. Some crackers, cheese, and crudités may prevent a riot before dinnertime.

Offer your guests a beverage as soon as they walk in the door. Let them know by the question what you have available. "Would you prefer soda, juice, or beer?" is a better question than, "Can I get you a drink?"

Serve dinner half an hour or so after your guests arrive. Linger over dessert and drinks as long as you like. The Folk will enjoy the conversation, even if they do not join in.

CHAPTER 35
THE GARDEN PARTY

The term "garden party" evokes an image of women in long dresses and ornate hats, an Edwardian fantasy of an estrogen-soaked British upper class. That must be due to the influence of the movies; I have neither given nor attended anything resembling it. Whatever the source of the image, it makes a garden party a good choice for a wedding reception, or any other party where you want to entertain a large number of people in a moderately formal setting. It is also a good choice for a dual-purpose party-for instance, for couples who would otherwise be divided into sports fans and sports widows. Instead of having a fans-only party, leaving spouses to their own devices, have a party for the nonfans in the yard, where the fans can join them when the game ends.

If you are going to serve a meal, you will need enough chairs and tables for everyone to sit down at once. These can be rented; look in the phone book under "Party Supplies." If you are serving only snacks and sweets, have enough seating for two-thirds of your guests, with an occasional table thrown in. Not having enough chairs for everyone causes a musical chairs effect, forcing people to mingle. Unless your guests are formally dressed or over forty years of age, stairways, the edges of raised decks, and bales of straw are perfectly acceptable seating options.

The garden party format is flexible enough to overlap several styles of entertaining. Given pleasant weather and adequate lighting, all parties tend to spill out into the garden. From the most formal tea to the most casual potluck, they all work well outside. The garden being the domain of the Folk, they will attend.

The logistics of a garden party at home are simple. You already know how the kitchen is arranged, how to access the garden from the kitchen, how much space you have available. If you are using rented tables, be sure that you have plenty of room around them, to allow your guests to circulate comfortably. If you do not have enough tablecloths to cover them, you will have to obtain them. These can be rented along with the tables, which can be fine, if you want to create a formal atmosphere. For a funkier look, pick up flat sheets inexpensively, or hem yardage from a fabric store. Do this several days in advance. It takes longer than one would think.

Disposable paper tablecloths tend to blow away. If you use them, weight them, either by putting heavy clips on the corners overhanging the edges of the tables, or by putting heavy flower arrangements along the length of the tables. Setting the tables with real china does not work for this purpose. After the meal, when the tables are cleared, the tablecloths will blow away.

Arrange the food buffet-style on a long table, if you are serving a full meal, or on several small ones, if you are serving snacks. Family-style service is too unwieldy to manage outdoors, where the kitchen is at a distance.

Garden parties in public places can be among the most elegant. Public parks and botanical gardens are large, and have the added benefit of having someone else to weed them. As the fairy blessings derived from entertaining cling to the locale, have the party in a place you frequent. Inquire about availability, costs, and amenities. Does the venue offer catering? Some require parties to use a caterer of the venue's choice. Is this acceptable?

Make friends with the resident Folk before the party, if possible. You need do no more than wander quietly about the garden, admiring the flowers. If you see a bird, a squirrel, or a lizard, tell it that you are going to have a party, and tell it to tell its friends. The word will get around.

Only throw a garden party when you can rely on good weather. This would be spring and fall in a hot climate, or summer in a cool one. Have shelter available, in case of rain or excessive sun. If you have a contingency plan in place for bad weather, the weather will be fine. This combines age-old principles of magic with modern faith in Murphy's Law.

Whatever choices you make, a garden party will automatically engage the attention of the Folk. It is in their territory.

CHAPTER 36
THE POTLUCK DINNER

In the most punctilious circles of society, potluck dinners do not exist. Potluck dinners are anathema, as there is no line separating host from guest. Chaos reigns.

Some people try to impose order on the potluck form by assigning dishes, or posting sign-up sheets for people to list their contributions. People who want to be sure of a balanced meal that conforms to their own aesthetic ideals should not involve themselves in potlucks. They should throw tidy little sit-down dinners, and provide everything themselves, as proper hosts.

In a potluck, you run the risk of having five kinds of spaghetti and six kinds of gelatin dessert. Each person involved brings whatever he or she chooses. That is where the *luck* comes in.

The natural habitat of the potluck supper is in clubs, churches, and offices. Ideal conditions for potluck formation include a large number of people who regard each other with an attitude of friendly competition. Showing off is highly desirable. If the group reflects a mix of cultures and ethnicities, the resulting meal can be an adventure. Every participant is equal in a potluck.

There are a couple of ways to modify the potluck form, to encourage group participation while providing a semblance of a wholesome meal. My friend Noel Wolfman provides a full meal, but specifies on the invitations that guests may bring desserts to share. This works perfectly. The guest-host relationship is preserved (and Noel is a singularly elegant hostess), everyone is assured of being well-fed, and there is the anticipation of an unknown dessert. Happy accidents can occur when things are not planned with pointillistic perfection. Who first discovered the symbiosis between chocolate and coffee? History is mute.

Another way to ensure a semblance of a balanced meal is for the host to provide the bare bones of a feast, and trust the guests for the baroque flourishes. If the host roasts a turkey and pops a package of rolls in the oven, Thanksgiving dinner may or may not occur, but everyone can at least have a sandwich. I adopted this habit when, for several years, I belonged to a group that was devoid of culinary vanity. A potluck dinner for twelve might consist of my offering plus eleven bags of potato chips. In retrospect, the potluck may not have been the best form for that group.

One important rule, when planning a potluck (if the term "planning" can be used with such a free form), is that each participant should bring only enough to serve eight people. As the numbers grow, truly impressive mountains of food can result, if this rule is not considered. It is elementary school math: if 50 people each bring enough food to feed 50 people, there will be 2,500 portions on the buffet table. The more people participate, the more variety is present, and the smaller the portions of each dish each person will take.

In any case, there will be plenty for the Folk.

CHAPTER 37
THE DESSERT BUFFET

The dessert buffet can be a tour de force by a single host, a cooperative event, or a competition. Any of them can be great fun.

Chocolate parties are as popular as chocolate itself. In some cases, one person makes six to ten desserts, which his or her guests sample. A chocolate party can also take the form of a cooperative potluck, or it can evolve into a cutthroat competition—cutthroat, that is, in the friendliest, most fun-loving way. A dear friend of mine throws a chocolate party annually on the Saturday nearest his birthday, as a way to encourage his friends to give him chocolate in lieu of other gifts. This annual party has become the most eagerly-anticipated event of the year. People work for months, perfecting their recipes, in order to win a stuffed toy or a cookbook. The quality of the offerings is stratospheric. Winners are chosen by ballot, with the host serving as tie-breaker. We all live on salads for weeks afterwards.

To be extra-thoughtful, have some nourishing food available in the kitchen. After sampling six or ten desserts, a salad and a bite of cheese can be a life-saver. Your guests will be grateful, when they think of the sugar hangover they would have suffered otherwise.

The Folk are not known to be partial to chocolate, but they are partial to festive occasions. *Do not* put leftovers from a chocolate party outside for the wildlife. As yummy as chocolate is for us, it is toxic for some other species. Keep the leftovers for yourself, or distribute them to your guests as they leave.

CHAPTER 38
THE AFTERNOON TEA

Nothing is as civilized as a cup of tea and a snack, taken in the afternoon in the company of friends. A century ago, a tea party was a ladies-only affair. The men were in another room, smoking cigars and drinking spirits. Today, anyone who cares to may drink tea, without calling his masculinity, or her femininity, into question.

A tea party is a way of entertaining a large group at small expense. This makes it ideal for wedding receptions, receptions in honor of out-of-town guests, retirement parties, graduation parties, and any other event for which the guest list may grow out of control. It can also become a way to entertain a small group more lavishly than you usually can. No rule says that you cannot make the little finger sandwiches with lobster salad, or top the canapés with caviar. Since it is the middle of the afternoon, you need not serve meal-sized portions, which helps make the lobster and caviar go a long way.

If you want to keep costs down, you must plan the party so that it does not intercept a mealtime. While, strictly speaking, tea time is somewhere between 4:00 and 5:00 P.M., you may certainly invite some friends over for tea any time after 2:00 P.M., as long as they will be gone by dinnertime. If they are still in residence at six o'clock, or certainly seven, you must give them three courses of something that is not only tasty, but filling.

You want to have good tea for a tea party. You will not find this at a grocery store, but at an import shop. Look for a British or Irish brand. If you are unsure of your choice, ask the proprietor for help. The proprietor is likely to be passionate about food and culture, and will be delighted to help you throw an authentic tea party. Loose tea is frequently of higher quality than that found in bags, and sure to enhance your reputation with those in the know. Good tea costs more than supermarket tea, but still only about twenty cents per cup. Your friends are worth it. The species of Folk known as the Gentry appreciate good tea, and will favor those who provide it.

To brew tea, begin by filling a kettle with fresh, cold water. Water that has been sitting in the water heater all day will have had all the dissolved oxygen cooked out of it. While only a connoisseur will be able to taste the difference, it is the connoisseur's taste that you are aiming to please. If your tap water tastes good enough to drink, it can be used to brew tea. If your tap water is not fit for drinking plain, use filtered or bottled water for your tea. Set the kettle on high heat to boil. When it boils, warm the pots by rinsing them with boiling water. For each cup of water that each pot holds, use one teaspoon of tea, plus an additional teaspoon, "for the pot." This extra teaspoon of tea serves as insurance against weak tea, which is always a faux pas. While many people like weak tea, it should be weak because it has not brewed for a long time, and not because insufficient leaves have been used. Pour the boiling water over the tea leaves in the pot.

A proper English pot of tea brews for a full five minutes. The hostess pours a small amount of milk into the cup as she serves, then follows with the tea. She asks, "One lump or two?" and hands the cup to her guest. This ritual does not work in every circle. Tea this strong requires milk, to make it easier on the stomach by buffering the acids. Most Americans prefer their tea weaker, with lemon. Unless you are more concerned with educating your guests than with entertaining them, begin pouring as soon as you add the water to the tea. Let the guests order themselves, according to how strong they like their tea. Let them flavor it themselves, with sugar or honey, and lemon or milk. Gently redirect any who attempt to use both lemon and milk; the result of this combination is little lumps of cheese floating in the tea.

How many people can you have to tea? To find the answer to this question, ask yourself how many teapots you have, how many tables and chairs, how many intimate friends. Your intimate friends do not have to make up your entire guest list. Their purpose is to serve as auxiliary hosts at the other tables. If you can persuade each of them to bring a teapot, you can entertain as many people at a formal tea as your space will hold.

The Afternoon Tea

For a very large tea party, formal service will prove impractical. Rent or borrow a large urn to bring the water to brewing temperature, and provide an assortment of teas for your guests to brew their own. In this case, use teabags. The snobs have already been turned off by the absence of a teapot on each table. If they have any manners, they will keep quiet. If they do not, you are better off without them.

To go with the tea, provide a variety of finger foods. Sweets are of the essence, dainty cookies and tarts, tiny scones. Have biscuits on the bland side, the better to go with lemon curd and marmalade. If your guests are hungry, and you want to encourage them to stay longer, serve savories as well. Any kind of sandwich is appropriate, as long as it can be picked up in one hand, and eaten in one or two bites. Tiny cream puffs filled with tuna salad are a delight.

The spread can be as elaborate as you care to make it. If you begin to bring out pastrami sandwiches and bottles of beer, however, your tea party is getting out of control. It has become a dinner party.

CHAPTER 39
THE MASQUERADE

If you want to throw a costume party for Halloween or Mardi Gras, all you have to do is put on the invitations the words "Costumes encouraged." Wearing costumes, substituting a fantasy identity for one's own, is a traditional part of these holidays. As noted in the Carnival section, the Folk take advantage of masked events to move among human beings. Getting your guests to wear costumes for Halloween or Mardi Gras is not a challenge.

For any other date, you will have to be more explicit in your instructions. The invitations should announce frankly, "A Costume Party!" Naming a theme can also inspire your friends' creativity. Knowing that they will be attending a vampire party or a sock hop will give them ideas for possible costumes.

Give prizes for coming in costume at all, as it is difficult for sensible adults to let their hair down. Give a better prize for the best costume, to be decided by vote among the guests. Mardi Gras beads cost pennies, but the stodgiest people will compete for them. Award beads for telling jokes, reciting poetry, playing pranks, bringing contributions to the dessert table, anything that adds to the success of the party.

Serve the food buffet-style, as some of the best costumes do not facilitate sitting shoulder to shoulder at a dining-room table. Serve only foods that are neat to eat, as dry-cleaning lace ruffs represents no inconsiderable expense. Serve no sloppy joes, and nothing à la marinara. You want these people to remain your friends at the end of the party.

CHAPTER 40
THE TELEVISION EVENT PARTY

While not everyone is a sports fan, every crowd has an event on television that means a lot to it. Some groups gather for the Big Game, others for an awards show or the season finale of a favorite series.

The person in the crowd with the biggest set is the natural host, if he or she also has room for everyone and is sociably inclined. These are intimate, informal occasions. Written invitations would be redundant, as these parties are usually arranged by consensus. The food should require little attention; serve nothing that requires elaborate dissection with knife and fork. For sporting events, serve chips and dips. Pizza or chili is a bonus. Add a selection of beers and sodas, and the menu is complete. The menu for other events can take its cue from the event itself. For an awards show, provide a buffet of canapés accompanied by champagne. Other events usually have within themselves the makings of "in" jokes, which are always best appreciated by the "in" group. For example, the hosts may decorate for a movie awards party using their favorite movie as the theme. Have a good time.

The Folk have not caught up with television yet, but they are always aware of sociability and food. When these are abundant, the Folk will attend.

CHAPTER 41
MISCELLANEOUS NOTES

INVITATIONS

The essential ingredients in an invitation are:

> The date, time, and address of the party

> The names of the hosts, and their phone numbers

> The type of party to which the guests are being invited

> The expected dress code, if that is not already implied by the type of party

Even if you think your guests know where you live, include the address. You may have forgotten that you have always socialized with one at her home. You may not know that another, who has been to your home several times, has always let someone else drive, and so has no clear idea how to get there on his own power.

You would be surprised to know how many people forget to put their own names on invitations. That is the single biggest factor in deciding whether to attend a party, so be sure to let your potential guests know who is throwing the party. They may have lost your phone number, so include it. Even if you do not need your guests to respond with their plans to attend, they might need to ask directions.

Your guests need to know what type of entertainment to expect. If you tell them it is a dinner party, they know to come hungry. If you tell them it is a bridal shower, they know to bring a present. If you tell them it is a potluck, they know to bring a casserole for eight. Scratch that-they probably do not know that. Specify, on an invitation for a potluck, that they should bring enough for eight servings of whatever they choose to make.

Some parties imply their own dress code. Pool parties imply casual clothes over bathing suits. Barbecues imply casual clothes without bathing suits. However, if you want people to wear formal clothing to a tea party, you will have to tell them.

TABLE SETTING

It is currently fashionable to treat the table as the most important element in a party's success. While it is nice to bring out Grandmama's china for a formal dinner once in a while, table setting is a minor art at most. If your friends are the sort of people who will eat your food and drink your wine, yet find fault with you over your tablecloth, you do not need them. Indeed, if your party is likely to be large and boisterous, Grandmama's china will be safest in the sideboard. Save it for the small, sit-down dinners with intimates, rather than taking chances with irreplaceable breakables in a crowd.

You have already decorated your home to suit your own taste. You have added such seasonal flourishes as appeal to you. You do not have to embellish your home further because you are having a party. Flowers are fine in the entry, and candles on the mantle, but if you have room for candles and flowers on the dining room table, you do not have enough food out.

Especially avoid the faddish use of platforms to elevate the serving dishes above the level of the table. One nudge may be enough to send thirty servings of jerk chicken crashing to the floor, along with the handmade platter they were served on. Ruined food and broken crockery never enhance a party, or a friendship. Plant your food firmly on the table. Not all your guests have the dexterity of jugglers.

NUMBERS

Two-thirds of the friends you invite will show up, whether or not you request them to respond. If fewer than two-thirds of the people you invite come to your parties, you may be inviting people who are not your friends. They may be colleagues, neighbors, or people you want to impress. They may be wonderful people who like you, but have not established a feeling of camaraderie with you yet. On the other hand, they may be good and faithful friends who can't attend because you are scheduling your parties badly. In the last half of December, most people have multiple commitments, with work, family, and several disparate social groups competing for their attention.

If more than two-thirds of the people you invite come to your parties, congratulate yourself. You are not only uncommonly popular, but you have established a reputation for throwing parties that are not to be missed.

AMOUNTS

Turkey serves one person per pound. Duck or goose serves one person per two pounds. Roast ham, beef, lamb, or pork serves two people per pound. Ground meat or sausages serve three people per pound. If you have more than one entrée, you can reduce the amounts of each individual one you need to serve.

This does not hold true for vegetarian alternatives. In my experience, most nonvegetarians will treat the vegetarian entrée as a side dish. They will take both the roast beef and the quiche. Therefore, have plenty of quiche available.

People tend to ignore soups and stews on buffet tables, so do not bother making them unless you are planning a sit-down dinner.

People also ignore cooked vegetables on buffet tables. This is so, even if their mothers raised them right. Serve salads and raw vegetables instead.

It is easier to have a dry party than to ferry your guests home at the end of the evening. If your friends are likely to overindulge, have a plan in place to keep them from driving. A chartered van or an extra bed might save the life of someone you love.

If an emergency prevents you from being host at your own party, but it is too late to notify your guests that the party is canceled, have your best friend take over as host. This is a sure way to identify your best friend: she is the one who is willing to do this. Of course, you already have the house clean and the food prepared. If you don't, you still have time to cancel the party. Asking your best friend to clean your house and cook dinner for forty, as well as to greet and entertain your other friends, is a sure way to divest yourself of a best friend.

AND FINALLY...

Does anyone expect you to throw parties for all the occasions I have listed? Absolutely not! Throwing more than two or three parties a year will cause people to take your hospitality for granted. They may start skipping your parties, figuring that they will catch the next one. Worse, some might think that you are trying to hog the limelight. Pick two or three times during the year on which to entertain. On the other holidays, let someone else do the hosting. Be a guest, or celebrate at home with your intimates. A quiet dinner at home with two or three close friends is worth all the parties in the world. It is in quiet, loving times that the Folk warm to us, and bless us.

PART IV
MORE LORE

PARTY TRADITIONS, BY HOLIDAY AND DATE

The purpose of this list is to give you a reason to throw the party you want, with full traditional justification. For instance, if you have an urge for fireworks in the autumn, you can announce a Diwali party, which also gives you a reason to put together a good vegetarian dinner and a killer poker tournament.

Important safety note: Please follow local ordinances regarding bonfires and fireworks! An hour of fun will not make up for a lifetime of guilt, if things get out of hand, and loss of life and property results. In addition, the Folk are merciless in regard to reminding people of the mistakes they have made in their lives.

BONFIRES:

Halloween—Orkney and the United States

May Eve—Sweden, Finland, and England

Midsummer Eve—Finland, Orkney

Guy Fawkes Day (November 5)—Britain, Orkney

St. Martin's Day (November 11)—Germany

Funkensonntag ("Spark Sunday," first Sunday in Lent)—Germany

New Year's Eve—Iceland

Twelfth Night (January 6)—Iceland, Germany

Yule—Orkney, Persia

All Hallows Day (November 1)—Orkney

Lammas (August 1)—Celtic Europe and the United States

FIREWORKS:

Diwali (late October or early November)—India

Nochebuena (Christmas Eve)—Mexico

Carnival (early spring)—Mazatlan

Guy Fawkes Day (November 5)—Britain

New Year's Eve—Puerto Rico, Ireland, Finland

Coptic Christmas (January 6 or 7)—Egypt

Christmas—Estonia, France, New Orleans

BREAKING TABOOS:

Halloween—United States

May Day—Germany

Day of the Oppressed Husband (Monday before Ash Wednesday)—Mexico

Saturnalia (December 25, January 1, or January 6)—France, Canada, ancient Rome

Kronia (July 30)—Greece (A harvest festival in honor of the god of agriculture.)

Carnival (January 6 until last Tuesday before Lent)—Worldwide, especially where Catholic influence is strong

PICNICS:

Cherry Blossom Viewing (late March to early April)—Japan

Coptic Christmas (January 6 or 7)—Egypt

Labor Day (first Monday in September)—United States

Christmas—Australia

PARADES:

Mardi Gras—Worldwide

Boxing Day (December 26)—Bahamas

St. Patrick's Day—Worldwide

New Year's Day—United States

Thanksgiving Day—United States

Independence Day—United States

FORTUNE TELLING:

Halloween—Ireland, United States

May Day—Europe, United States

Midsummer—Finland

Christmas—Scotland, Russia, Germany, Spain

Christmas Eve—Poland

COOKING TERMS AND ABBREVIATIONS

tsp: teaspoon

Tbsp: tablespoon

A la marinara: with tomato sauce

Cream: soften fat with beater or spoon until fluffy

Crudités: raw vegetables

Farina: fine grained wheat cereal, of the Cream of Wheat type

Flour: unless otherwise specified, all-purpose, white wheat flour

Fruitcake mix: no one knows

Mole: literally means "sauce," refers to complex sauces originating in the Mestizo culture of Mexico

Nonreactive: made out of a substance that is not chemically affected by the presence of acid. Stainless steel, glass, ceramic, and enamel are nonreactive. Cast iron and aluminum are not.

Sauté: cook in a very hot skillet with a small amount of oil, while moving food constantly by stirring or shaking pan

Scald: heat to just below the boiling point

Simnel cake: a rich fruitcake decorated with marzipan

Treacle: molasses

Venison: deer meat

NAMES FOR THE FAIR FOLK

Gentle Folk

Fair Folk

Gentle People

Good Folk

Good Neighbors

The Gentry

GENERAL GLOSSARY

Apsaras: beautiful female water spirits, known for their skill at love-making

Bacchantes: female devotees of Bacchus, the god of revelry

Bogies, boggles, bugs, and bugbears: various names for mischievous, or unfriendly, beings, who may or may not be imaginary

Brownies: helpful beings who live in or near rural homesteads

Cascarones: empty eggshells, filled with confetti

Cybelle: an ancient southern European mother goddess

Demeter: Greek goddess of grain and agriculture

Dowry: money provided by a bride's family for the support of the bride during her marriage

Elf-spirit: being of northern Europe

Faerie: the country of the Fair Folk, usually located underground

Finmen: the fathers and husbands of the mermaids, actively hostile to human beings

Glamour: the ability of the Folk to make things appear different than they are

Gremlins: mischievous beings who cause mechanical or electronic machines to fail

Hades: Greek god of wealth and the realm of the dead

The Hunger: the Irish Potato Famine, late 1840s

Knockers: Folk who work in coal mines

Lakshmi: Hindu goddess of prosperity

Lent: forty days leading up to Easter

Leprechaun: Irish shoemaker Folk

Lugh: Celtic god of light

Marmots: groundhogs

Mermaids: female sea-people, half human, half fish. Their relationships with human beings are ambivalent.

Mestizo: mixed, especially referring to a mix of Spanish and Native American

Mistletoe: parasitic plant that lives in trees. Sacred in pre-Christian Europe.

Nisse: Norwegian house elf

Odin: Chief god of the Norse pantheon

Palm Sunday: the Sunday before Easter

Paschal: pertaining to Easter

Peries: fire-spirits of northern England, visible as the Aurora Borealis

Persephone: Greek goddess of youth and springtime

Pomona: Roman goddess of orchards

Quinceanera: a girl's fifteenth birthday, celebrated as a coming of age. Also, the girl herself, on the occasion of her fifteenth birthday.

Reindeer Elf: hairy little man who protects domestic reindeer

Reindeer Fairy: primal mother of the Sami people, who gives fertility and prosperity

Rhea: mother of the Greek gods

Rusalki: seductive water spirits native to Russia

Salamander: the elemental spirit of fire

Santería: polytheistic African religion, practiced in the southern United States and Latin America. Also called voudoun or espirtismo.

Selkies: the seal people of Celtic and Norse regions

Sidhe: the people of the hills, the Irish Fair Folk

Star Maidens: beautiful young women of Native American legend, who come from the heavens

Swan Maidens: Folk native to Australia, in the form of beautiful young women with the wings of swans

Tomte: Swedish house elf

Wild Hunt: spirits riding through the sky on winter nights

Wotan: British name for Odin

Yule Cat: a gigantic cat, native to Iceland, who hunts and eats people who wear old clothes on Christmas

Zeus: chief god of the Greek pantheon

RECIPE LIST